Morris,

Thanks for your
encouragement, friendship
& support,

In the Grip
of His Grace,

Just

CHRONICLES FROM
THE CROSSROADS OF
CONEHATTA, CEREBRAL PALSY AND THE CROSS

JUSTIN FISHER

Cover design by Nathan Preg. Cover photography by Wendy Ware

(Chronicles from the Crossroads of) Conehatta, Cerebral Palsy & the Cross
c – 2014 by Justin Fisher
Published by CreateSpace.com
part of the Amazon.com family

Library of Congress Cataloging-in-Publication Data

Fisher, Justin
        Conehatta, cerebral palsy & the cross.

ISBN-13: 978-1497439078
ISBN-10: 1497439078

<u>**DEDICATION**</u>

To the whole Fisher Family:
Big Bill, Momma Fay, Sharm & Cody B.
(plus all of the inlaws, outlaws, nieces and
nephews). Thank you so much for your
love, encouragement and support.

ACKNOWLEDGEMENTS

"For from Him and through Him and for
Him are all things.
To Him be the glory forever! Amen."
Romans 11:36

Special Thanks To:
Contributing authors **Donna Howell** and
Sharman Fisher Malone

My ace editorial staff: **Fay Fisher**, **Tommy
Battles**, and **Quinn Hill**

Thanks for making me look good;
Cover designer, **Nathan Preg**.
Cover photography, **Wendy Ware**.

*God brings people into our lives for a
season and a reason…This books is, at
least in part, a testimony to that.*

Table of Contents

Foreward
by Donna Howell

*T*his story really begins several months
before it begins. I belong to a great singles group
at my home church. We are tight knit and very
active. Several years ago while driving to our
monthly "Game-night Get-Together", I heard the
local Christian radio station, WDJC, advertising
their annual singles cruise. It was scheduled for
four days in the Yucatan Peninsula in August
2005. Since one of the DJ's sponsoring the
event, Carrie Cates, was in our singles group, I
decided to try to stir up some interest. When I
arrived at the party, I told the gang about the
cruise, and quickly had several who were very
interested.

One of the interested parties was my pal,
Justin Fisher. Justin had joined our group about a
year prior, and, despite his disability, he was very
active in virtually everything we did. Justin, or

"Hoss" as I call him, has cerebral palsy, but he doesn't let it slow him down. Justin had also taught our Sunday school class several times, and when Carrie discovered he was coming on the cruise, she invited him to be the speaker at our chapel service.

Because of this high profile role during the service, and because the wheelchair makes Justin immediately recognizable, he became somewhat of a celebrity on the ship. (It also didn't hurt that Justin did a stirring rendition of the Ray Stevens' classic "Ahab the Arab" in the karaoke lounge on the first night of the cruise!) You couldn't get on the elevator without a gaggle of people unloading and stopping to talk to Justin.

Our singles group was large in numbers and several had been able to come along for the trip. This crew always had fun together, and the cruise turned into one big party. We settled in the vacation mode quickly and the first night at dinner I heard Hoss mention he would love to snorkel if the onshore event could handle his handicap. I made note of the conversation but tucked it away in the back of my mind. Because of the limitations of his disability, I wasn't even sure the idea was a good one to begin with.

Several of us disembarked the next day to visit the sites and sounds of another country and I noticed the tourist events posted. I thought of Justin and the snorkeling idea. We were walking around the shopping area at the port and I asked Justin if he still wanted to snorkel. He said he did.

I grew up in Baldwin County, AL near the Gulf of Mexico. I have always been comfortable around water especially the ocean. I am an avid scuba diver, a water skier, and a one-time lifeguard in Gulf Shores, Alabama. I remember thinking, "Why not?". So off I went to investigate the snorkeling option available to tourists at this port.

The outdoor activity coordinators were at small desks with thatched roofs to give off an authentic island look to the tourist. I spoke with the gentleman stationed there and explained that I wanted to help my friend with cerebral palsy to enjoy this activity. The coordinator did not seem concerned and agreed that the boat operator would help me with Justin's unique challenges. I returned to the shopping center and told Justin we were all set.

Our friend Kimmie decided she wanted to tag along. (I think partly for the fun and partly to see how in the *world* I was going to tactically and logistically pull this off!) The activity coordinator acquired a taxi for us and after Justin asked some brief questions to satisfy his curiosity as to whether or not he would be able to snorkel, Kimmie assisted him with his crutches and started walking towards the small passenger van.

Justin uses a big power wheelchair that was going to have to be left at the thatched roof kiosk in the care of the coordinator. With Kimmie helping Justin into the taxi, I hopped onto his wheelchair to safely park it between the small booths in the customer activity area. Now, I had never operated a motorized wheelchair. It had a small joy stick on the arm rest for Justin to maneuver himself around. I pulled back on the joystick to operate the vehicle in reverse, raced backwards at a surprisingly fast speed and promptly slammed directly into the booth!

This sent the event coordinator into a full sprint towards me with a frightened look. I could tell that he was not concerned for my safety or for the safety of the wheelchair. No, he was worried I was going to reduce his little thatched roof booth to shreds. I calmly stated, "I got this.", very gently moved the joystick forward, very gently inched away from the thatched booth and then very violently slammed into the booth again! It may or may not have been tilted slightly off the ground and three inches back from its original location when the earth stopped shaking. And I may or may not have left his little thatched roof booth with the distinctive slash marks left by a wheelchair tire from my attempt to be a designated driver

With the event coordinator thoroughly disgusted with me, I then decided to exit the wheelchair to try maneuvering while standing next to it. This worked a great deal better and I finally parked it between the two booths. The event coordinator looked relieved that I was no longer driving the wheelchair and I got the distinct feeling he wanted to comment on women drivers. However, he was polite and handed me a ticket for our snorkeling excursion. He pointed me to the taxi, and left me with only one instruction, "Ask for Pedro."

I entered the front passenger seat of the taxi and started a casual conversation with the driver about his life and the area we were traveling. He revealed he was not Mexican but Mayan. He could trace his family lineage back to the era of the conquistadors. He took control of the conversation to complain how the Mexicans had taken over his homeland and destroyed the Mayan way of life. He literally spoke about four paragraphs without taking a breath. Now, I am not a historian, but I remember from my World History class in the tenth grade that the Mayan Empire declined in the 1500s. But this guy acted as if it happened last week. He was still fired up about it!

When we reached our destination, Kimmie helped Justin out of the taxi while I paid the driver and exited to find our guide, Pedro. There were two short piers, extending out to the ocean from the beach but there was not a boat anywhere in sight. Having in no other options, I followed the instructions given to me. I called out, "Pedro!", and, evidently that's a common name in those parts, 'cause at once five guys started towards me!

I was a little taken aback but I showed them the ticket. They spoke some short phrases to each other in Spanish, then turned and walked away! This did not help me find Pedro, so I protested in English and they answered me in Spanish and pointed to one of the piers. I got the point. Evidently, *my* Pedro was out on the water with a snorkeling group and would soon return.

Justin, Kimmie, and I headed towards the pier to wait. It was a small stretch of beach but it was a long stretch of sand. You know how your feet sink into the sand a little when you walk on the beach? Well, crutches have a smaller surface area than feet, and they sink deeper. It was painful for us watching and for Justin walking, but we worked our way across the sand and the three of us settled onto the beach to wait.

Within about fifteen minutes, a small skiff came around the end of the cove headed towards our pier and spot on the beach. The skiff contained two Hispanic gentlemen at the motor end and about six tourists. I inquired of the driver, "Pedro?" and to my relief, he nodded.

I explained our situation and he spoke to the other gentleman. They assisted Justin into the skiff. The other gentleman grabbed snorkeling gear for the three of us and off we went. We traveled out of the cove and around a point of land that jutted out of the mainland. He slowed the boat over a small reef and killed the engine. I decided the best course of action for this adventure was for me to get into the ocean and have Pedro and his friend lower Justin into the water.

This area had no current so I thought it would be perfect for our adventure. With Hoss floating in the ocean beside me, however, I soon decided this excursion might have a higher level of difficultly than I had anticipated. See, Justin does not have the best motor skills and independently all he was able to do was lie in the water floating on his back. I finally got him upright and gave him some quick instructions on how to snorkel so he would be comfortable.

However, I forgot to explain how to clear a snorkel. Justin had been on his back for a couple minutes so as I flipped him forward to put his face in the water, he immediately started coughing and choking. I got him upright again and pulled the snorkel out of his mouth and stupidly said, "What is the problem?" Justin sputtered, "There is water in the snorkel! I can't breathe!" Now, my dual reaction, as is often the case on adventures with Justin, was first of embarrassment and then laughter.

I told Justin, "my bad" and then explained how to clear the snorkel. With the snorkel clear of water and back in place in Justin's mouth, I flipped him forward again with his face in the water. I held him there a minute and heard the sound of his breathing through the snorkel. It was a bit like an old cassette audio recording of Darth Vader but I could tell his breathing was normal and had a natural rhythm to it. I asked Kimmie to hand me a mask and snorkel and then proceeded to move Justin along the reef and away from the boat.

I was not prepared for the next twenty to thirty minutes. In all the preparation of this adventure, I had worried about his handicap and my ability to make this work. I had not considered his reaction to an activity he had never experienced. I worked our way over small schools of fish and plant life that was bursting with color. Purple seaweeds, yellow and red coral, and bright neon blue fish were vibrant in the shallow water below us. I could hear Justin giggling into the snorkel beside me.

Some of the sea weeds were growing up about three to four feet off the ocean floor and were within reach of the surface. I moved Justin close to one and he reached out and touched it. There it was again …that giggle. I then heard a muffled "Donna" and so I stopped and up righted myself and then Justin. I pulled the snorkel from his mouth and Justin stated, "I want to see you swim to the ocean floor and touch the sand and some stuff. I can't do that but I can watch you."

I have to pause here to say that this comment more than put a lump in my throat. I had been on so many scuba dives and ocean swims and, I must confess, I have never considered how precious it was to be able to perform these tasks. I got Justin settled back in the water face down. I took a deep breath and swam down to the floor of the ocean and stirred the sand. I dazzled Justin with somersaults and brought some sea shells up for him to view.

Within a few minutes, Pedro pulled up next to us. Our time was up. Pedro and his shipmate got Justin back in the boat, I climbed in, and then we all headed back to the cove. Upon docking, we discovered that we only had about twenty-five minutes to get back to the cruise ship or we would have to make the small fishing village our new address. I stressed this to Pedro and he sent his shipmate to the main road to hail us a taxi.

Pedro then called to a couple of the guys on the beach and they picked Justin up to carry him to the taxi since his journey on his crutches would take entirely too long. Kimmie and I gathered our towels and things and then laughed histerically at Justin being carried to the taxi. Justin who has never ceased to use his handicap to his advantage was singing as he was being carried through the village convincing the locals that he was not handicapped but probably just intoxicated. I'm not certain, but he may have slurred, "I ain't drunk. Put me down!"

We made it to the taxi and back to port in time and continued our cruise. It still blows me away that Justin put complete trust in the fact that I would take care of him that day on the ocean. I have since dared myself to have that kind of abandonment with God and my life. It has caused me to ask myself who was more handicapped in the water that day? I was numb and blind to the wonderment of God's creation in the ocean. My friend was not.

Vacations must always come to an end and this one ended over ten years ago. I, however, have never forgotten that day. I thought I would help a friend out who wanted an adventure beyond the limits of his handicap. What I found was a friend helping me learn a lesson in blessings and about the things I take for granted. The sound of that child-like giggle in the snorkel has stayed in my head all these years. I am grateful to God for the wonderment we can experience as adults just as we did as children. We only need to disown our handicaps.

From HATE To LOVE

Riddle Me This

I love a good mystery. In my opinion, that's what really drives a good book, movie or television show. My wife, Kelly, and I enjoy watching the "Dateline" murder mysteries. We've recently discovered the British crime drama "Sherlock", a modern take on Sir Authur Conan Doyle's character. I could go on and on with a list of guilty pleasures including "Lost", "Prison Break" and "24". I'll just stop there and say most of the programs we enjoy together have some element of mystery.

Did you know that the Gospel of Jesus is a mystery? In fact, the Apostle Paul uses the word translated "mystery" no less than sixteen times in his New Testament letters, including seven times in the Book of Ephesians that only has six chapters. Let's take note of a few of them.

- This mystery is *personal.* Ephesians 1:9 reads, "(God) made known to us the *mystery of his will* according to *his* good pleasure, which *he* purposed in Christ." Can you imagine? The God of the universe has made known to us insignificant, finite beings His plans, His pleasures, His purposes…

- This mystery is *protected.* Ephesians 3:9 reads, "And to make plain to everyone the administration of *this mystery, which for ages past was kept hidden* in God, who created all things." Shhhh. It *was* a secret, but now we can shout it from the housetops! Why? Because God has revealed it to us through His Son, Christ Jesus.

- This mystery is *profound*. Ephesians 5:32 reads, "This is a *profound mystery*—but I am talking about Christ and the church." Deep enough so that some of the most brilliant men to ever walk the planet couldn't get their minds around it…yet simple enough for a child to understand.

- This mystery is approached *prayerfully*. Ephesians 6:19 & 20b reads, "*Pray* also for me, that whenever I speak, words may be given me so that I will fearlessly make known *the mystery of the gospel… Pray* that I may declare it fearlessly, as I should." These are the verses I often post on my Facebook page before a speaking engagement…a reminder that this mystery remains unsolved without divine intervention.

Winston Churchill is quoted in a radio broadcast from October 1939 as having said, "I cannot forecast to you the action of Russia. It is a riddle, wrapped in a mystery, inside an enigma." And that's what the Gospel of Christ is. So, just for giggles, I thought we'd use a riddle to help us solve this mystery.

Here's the challenge…On the next page is a riddle. Change ONLY ONE letter of the word per line to MAKE A NEW WORD ON EACH LINE (no proper names) to transition from "HATE" to "LOVE".

HATE

— — — —

— — — —

— — — —

LOVE

We Gotta Start Somewhere
(Dealing with this little thing called HATE.)

*A*nd contrary to popular belief, we must start here. We must start with the word "hate". I personally believe that it does no good to tell someone how much the God of the universe loves them, until they are told how much we are naturally inclined to hate Him. Romans 8:7- 8 says, "The mind governed by the flesh is *hostile* to God; it does not submit to God's law, nor can it do so. Those who are in the realm of the flesh cannot please God." The King James Version of the Bible translates the word "enmity". It's the same word used in Genesis 3:15 when God says to the serpent "And I will put enmity between you and the woman…"

Because I like to hunt, and because I have some good camouflage, I have gotten up close to various types of animals in the woods over the years. I've gotten within crossbow shooting distance of deer, hogs and turkey. I've gotten within spitting distance of birds, squirrels, mice, and at least one armadillo. But I've never had an experience with a snake. In fact, the first experience I have in the woods by myself with a snake may just be my last time hunting. Why? Because I hate 'em! That's mine, and I think most people's, natural default setting.

And that's our default setting in our attitude towards God. We are hostile. We are at enmity. We hate Him. In Romans 5:10, Paul writes, "…while we were God's enemies, we were reconciled to him…" You might say "But, Justin, when I was little, my parents taught me to love God, and I've always loved God." Dear friends, if you say that you love God because you've *always* loved God, then I'm afraid you've never fully realized the depravity of your sins.

Then some of you might say, "But, Justin, in my *heart* I don't feel like I hate God." And there is indeed a popular world-view that simply says, "Follow your heart." The problem with that is that Jeremiah 17:9 says, *"The heart is deceitful* above all things, and *desperately wicked*: who can know it?" Following your heart will get you into trouble.

You know what the bottom line is? The bottom line is: we just want to do what pleases us! Paul even tells us in Romans 8:5a,"Those who live according to the flesh have their minds set on what the flesh desires." Which is the Biblical equivalent of comedian Wanda Sykes monologue "I'ma Be Me". "Well," you might ask, "What's wrong with that?" Funny you should ask. Paul gives us the answer in the next verse, Romans 8:6a, "The mind governed by the flesh is *death*." That's why the following verses, quoted at the beginning of this chapter, say that we *do not* and we *cannot* please God. Why? Because we are dead! And that "deadness" puts us in direct opposition, hatred, towards God, who is life!

Jesus says in John 14:15, "If you love me, keep my commands." And I really believe that if we are not following His commands, then we're not truly loving Him. And what is the opposite of love?

Death and Taxes
(Change the "H" to a "D" to go from HATE to DATE.)

*T*here's a couple different ways we need to approach this idea of a date. First of all there's a date looming out there for all of us. Hebrews 9:27 says, "Just as people are *destined to die once*, and after that to face judgment." There are indeed two certainties in this life; death and taxes. (I teach Macroeconomic Policy in my classes...so don't get me started on taxes!) "If the Lord tarries" we will indeed all die.

So in light of the previous chapter, we *are* all dead, and we *will* all die. And if we die while dead in our sins and hating the God who created us, then face His righteous judgment, how do you think that's gonna work out? Well, I've got three words for you; NOT. TO. GOOD! So at some point in our lives we realize that a) we're in a hate relationship with God -He hating our sins, and us hating Him- and that b) we will one day die and face His judgment. And our natural tendency is to get ready for *that* date like we get ready for all our other dates.

Now it's been awhile since I was single and dating, but I remember what it was like to get ready for a big date. You gotta shave, shower and shampoo. You gotta put on your black cowboy boots and your black button down shirt with the sleeves rolled up. Gotta get some product in your hair...like you like it! (Maybe all that's just me.) Even as old married folks, Kelly and I have tried to make dating each other a priority, and we still try to look nice for each other. Though I promise, she does a *much* better job at that than I do.

In a similar way, people try to "clean themselves up" before their big date with God. We try to be good and look good and feel good and act good...but it's no good. Isaiah 64:6 says "All of us have become like one who is *unclean*, and *all our righteous acts are like filthy rags*; we all shrivel up like a leaf, and like the wind our sins sweep us away." Now we've got a bag of old rags that we keep in the laundry closet to clean up spills and such. They're tattered and stained, and we might think this verse is referring to something like that when describing the righteousness of our self-help date prep. But the reality is much worse.

Our pastor at New Prospect Missionary Baptist Church during my high-school years was Brother Reggie Williams, who is now the Director of the Scott County Mississippi Baptist Association. I remember him explaining this "filthy rags" analogy one time. He explained that in the middle ages there was this terrible disease called leprosy. It was very painful, with oozing sores, and very contagious. So contagious in fact, that when people who had the disease walked through villages they were required to yell out, "Unclean, unclean, unclean!" to warn everyone not to get near them.

Many times they congregated in what was called leper colonies. As the sores burst open and the puss from them oozed, the lepers would seek some small solace in wiping their wounds. Without modern medicine or even modern hygiene in these colonies, discarded pieces of cloth were all that could be used. Since everyone in the colony already had the disease there was no fear of contamination. So, as not to be wasteful, the lepers would wipe their sores, and then hang the rags on poles to dry and be used by others in their same condition.

Can you image? Can you fathom the foul, filthy, putrid condition of these rags? Quite honestly, anything I can imagine probably does not come close. But these images do get our minds thinking in the right direction when it comes to how futile even our best efforts are to clean ourselves up for our date with an infinitely holy God. And the real mystery of the Gospel is that there's no reason to try to get yourself clean, because God dotes on you already!

God's Refrigerator
(Change the "A" to an "O" to go from DATE to DOTE.)

*N*ow, you may not believe this, but dote *is* a real word. It's not a commonly used word in this day and age, but it's a real word. Meriam-Webster defines <u>dote</u> as "lavish or excessive in one's attention, fondness or affection". I'll use it in a sentence for you. "I absolutely dote on my wife." Sometimes I'll call Kelly and say, "Baby, are your legs tired?...'Cause you been running around in my mind *all* day long!" (She *loves* it when I say things like that, too.)

The first time I remember hearing the word "dote" was in what I consider to be the greatest western movie of all time, Larry McMurtry's "Lonesome Dove". In one of the sub-plots, Jake Spoon has accidently shot and killed the mayor of Fort Smith, Arkansas, Benny Johnson. Benny's widow, Peach, bullies the sheriff, July Johnson (who by the way is also

Benny's brother) into pursuing "that murderin' Jake Spoon". A few days later, Peach shows back up at the Sheriff's Office to tell the deputy, Roscoe Brown (don't you love these names!) that July's wife, Elmira, has "done run off".

> Roscoe: Well, Peach, July left for Texas six days ago.
> Peach: Well, surely you can find Texas, Roscoe!
> Roscoe: I can find Texas, but how do I find July?
> Peach: Now, Roscoe, Elmira ain't hardly worth it, but July *dotes* on that woman.

I must draw the obvious analogy here: we ain't hardly worth it but God *dotes* on us!

In Psalm 139:16-18 King David paints a beautiful picture of this sentiment when he says of God:

> "Your eyes saw my unformed body;
> all the days ordained for me were written
> in your book before one of them came to

be. *How precious to me are your thoughts, God! How vast is the sum of them! Were I to count them, they would outnumber the grains of sand—* when I awake, I am still with you."

If God had a refrigerator your picture would be on it! And that's where this whole thing turns scandalous! Why? Because the infinitely holy God of the universe would certainly have to stoop down in order to dote on us dead humans with our filthy self-righteousness. Notice the words of Paul in Phillipians 2:6-8 as he penned:

"(Christ Jesus), being in very nature God,
   did not consider equality with God something
to be used to his own advantage;
 rather, *he made himself nothing*
   by taking the very nature of a servant *(a slave),*
   being made in human likeness.
And being found in appearance as a man,
   he humbled himself
   by becoming obedient to death—
      even death on a cross!"

Can you imagine! The holy and *righteous* only Son of God became a slave, so that we, the *unrighteous* slaves of sin and the flesh might become the sons and daughters of God. Simply scandalous!

I have a "Yahoo!" e-mail account, and when I log-out I'm instantly directed to their homepage where the headlines seem to always be filled with the scandal of the day. The topics include "Who's cheating who, and who's being true, and who don't even care anymore." (Thanks Charly McClain.) And one of the most scandalous pairings ever, at least in my mind, was when Julia Roberts married Lyle Lovett.

When I was in high school, I thought Julia was the most beautiful woman on the planet. And if you don't know who Lyle Lovett is, Google him if you dare! I know that we're all created in the image of God, but let's just say that Lyle has not yet received a glorified body...or face for that matter! The only solace this union brought me was that if Julia could marry Lyle, then love truly was blind and there was hope for all of us! But here's my point, compared to the ugliness of our sin, Lyle Lovett looks like Brad Pitt. And compared to the glory, holiness and beauty of God, Julia Roberts looks like Honey Boo-Boo's Mamma!

These thoughts force us to contemplate Paul's three questions in Romans 8:31-32:

1. "What, then, shall we say in response to these things?"
2. "If God is for us, who can be against us?"

3. "He who did not spare his own Son, but gave him up for us all—how will he not also, along with him, graciously give us all things?"

God dotes on us, and He bids us come, and make peace with Him.

Peace Out
(Change the "T" to a "V" to go from DOTE to DOVE.)

"*W*hen the *dove* returned to him in the

evening, there in its beak was a freshly plucked

olive leaf! Then Noah knew that the water had

receded from the earth."(Genesis 8:11) It's no

coincidence that the dove and the olive branch

are the international symbols of peace. Why?

Because Noah knew that God's righteous wrath

was complete...now there could be peace.

We all want peace, don't we? Kelly has

told me that she has come to loathe the process of

bedtime at our house. "It's time for bed. Put

down the X-box controller. Turn off the Kindle.

Go put pajamas on. Brush your teeth. Go potty."

These are simple instructions to simple tasks that

even young children like ours should be able to

follow. But there is always the wailing and

gnashing of teeth. You'd think we were asking

the children to scale the south face of Everest or something!

But when it's all over, there is peace. Now, Mom and Dad may feel like they've been part of storming the beaches at Normandy, but with overwhelming victory comes peace. There is, however, another reference to peace and a dove that may even more appropriately embody the essence of our transitional riddle.

It is recorded in Matthew 3:16, "As soon as Jesus was baptized, he went up out of the water. At that moment heaven was opened, and he saw the Spirit of God descending like a *dove* and alighting on him." The Prince of Peace has come! He has come to reconcile the hostility and *hate* between us and God. He has come to warn us of the impending *date* of judgment (Matthew 12:36). He has come to tell us that God *dotes* on us. And He has come to let us know that the same Spirit that descended from Heaven like a *dove* can live inside you!

That's why Paul said in Colossians that, through Jesus, God "reconciled to himself all things, whether on earth or in heaven, making *peace* by the blood of his cross." Then notice how Paul really drives this point home in Romans 8:9-15.

"You, however, are not in the realm of the flesh but are in the realm of *the Spirit*, if indeed the *Spirit of God lives in you*. And if anyone does not have the *Spirit of Christ*, they do not belong to Christ. *But if Christ is in you*, then even though your body is subject to death because of sin, *the Spirit* gives life because of righteousness. *And if the Spirit of him who raised Jesus from the dead is living in you*, he who raised Christ from the dead will also give life to your mortal bodies because of *his Spirit who lives in you*. Therefore, brothers and sisters, we have an obligation—but it is not to the flesh, to live according to it. For if you live according to the flesh, you will die; but if by *the Spirit* you put to death the misdeeds of the body, you will live. For those who are led by *the Spirit* of God are the children of God. *The Spirit* you received does not make you slaves, so that you live in fear again; rather, *the Spirit* you received brought about your adoption to sonship. And by him we cry, "*Abba,* Father."

"Abba, Father" is loosely translated into Conehatta, Mississippi English as "Daddy, God." Can I tell you that at this stage of my life there may be no greater joy than when my children meet me at the front door or come running off the school bus screaming "Daddy! Daddy! Daddy!" This is why I believe that in Matthew 19:26 when "Jesus looked at them and said, '*With man this is impossible*, but with God all things are possible'," it wasn't a condemnation, but an invitation.

He wasn't saying, "You worthless kids! You never do anything right, and you'll never amount to anything!" No. He was extending the olive branch, through the person of the Holy Spirit, who invites us to come and find peace. It's an invitation to come and be loved.

Nary a One
(Change the "D" to an "L" to go from DOVE to LOVE.)

A couple chapters ago I taught you the word "dote", now I'll teach you another – "nary". "Nary" according to Meriam-Webster is defined as "not one". My Dad taught me this word. He might have used it in a sentence like, "So and so survived the accident with *nary* a scratch." I think this a useful word to attempt to answer the rhetorical questions Paul asks at the end of the eighth chapter of Romans. "Who shall separate us from the *love* of Christ? Shall trouble or hardship or persecution or famine or nakedness or danger or sword?"

Nary a soul. Nary a circumstance. Nary a thing. Paul says as much himself in the following verses. "No, in all these things we are *more than conquerors* through Him who loved us." It's almost as if Paul wanted to invent a new word. "We're conquerors…but we're *more* than that!" I've heard people say more than happy, more than satisfied, even more than helpful. But more than conquerors is just outside of my imagination. And that's because Paul's trying to use human words to describe a spiritual reality.

So he wraps up the chapter this way, "For I am convinced that neither death nor life, neither angels nor demons, neither the present nor the future, nor any powers, neither height nor depth, nor anything else in all creation, will be able to separate us from the *love* of God that is in Christ Jesus our Lord."

Nary a thing! Enough said.

Just a Second in 2nd Corinthians

Comfort in Suffering

*A*fter a brief salutation, Paul begins his second letter to the church at Corinth with these heartfelt words: "Praise be to the God and Father of our Lord Jesus Christ, the Father of compassion and the God of all *comfort*, who *comforts* us in all our troubles, so that we can *comfort* those in any trouble with the *comfort* we ourselves receive from God. For just as we share abundantly in the sufferings of Christ, so also our *comfort* abounds through Christ. If we are distressed, it is for your *comfort* and salvation; if we are *comforted*, it is for your *comfort*..."

Now that's comfortable, ain't it? It reminds of a story that the great Mississippi comedian, Jerry Clower, used to tell about getting comfortable. He said he was in a particular town to do a show, and he checked into the hotel early. He checked into the hotel early because Alabama and Nebraska were playing football that afternoon, and he wanted to get in front of the TV and watch Bear Bryant's boys whoop-up on the Cornhuskers. Jerry's plan for ultimate comfort was to "put on the loose fittin' pajamas, and fix it to where that air-conditioning vent would blow up one britches leg and down the other."

But before we get too caught up on the comfort, let us backtrack a little then add another verse or two. 2 Corinthians 1:5-7 reads, "For just as we share abundantly in the *sufferings* of Christ, so also our comfort abounds through Christ. If we are *distressed*, it is for your comfort and salvation; if we are comforted, it is for your comfort, which produces in you patient endurance of the same *sufferings* we *suffer*. And our hope for you is firm, because we know that just as you share in our *sufferings*, so also you share in our comfort." I think the lesson is clear:

these verses are just as much about suffering as they are about comfort. The two go in hand in hand.

At this point you might be thinking, "Why did you have to go there? Why couldn't you just stop with the comfort part?" It is true. For so many of us our main goal is our comfort. Our comfort has become our god. It is the one thing that prevents us from totally "selling out" and following Christ.

I once heard Texas native and comedian, Ron White, tell a story about being comfortable. It goes something like this: "I was sitting on a bean-bag chair in my underwear in the middle of the day eating Cheetos…and I'm flipping through the channels when this televangelist, Robert Tilton, comes on the TV. He's staring at me and we begin this conversation:

Tilton: Are you lonely?

Ron: (looking at his stated setting….)
       Yep.

Tilton: Have you wasted half your life in
         bars pursuing sins of the flesh?

Ron: Wow. This guy's good.

Tilton: Are you sitting in a bean-bag chair
         in your underwear in the middle of
         the day eating Cheetos?

Ron: (trembling with a shaky voice…)
       Yeeeessssssiirrr!

Tilton: Do you feel the urge to get up and
         send me $1,000?

Ron: Close! Whew. For a second there I
       thought he was talking to me!"

Why does Ron "bail out" at this point?
Well, it's because if he were truly convinced that
God, through Tilton, were speaking specifically
to him, then he'd have to take action. More
specifically, he'd have to give something up.

Firstly, he'd have to give up the $1,000. Then, to become a fully devoted Christ follower, he'd have to give up his rebellious lifestyle and deny himself. Could he do it under his own power? No, none of us can. What would induce this type of change? It's recognizing the beauty and the power and the majesty of the Cross. But, Ron, like so many of us when challenged with something difficult, balks…like a calf starring at a new gate.

It's the same sentiment reflected in Acts 26:28, "Then Agrippa said to Paul, 'You almost persuade me to become a Christian'." (NKJV) We're all in for the peace, and love, and joy, and comfort, and good happiness stuff. But when it comes to suffering…that's when we pull up short. But in the first chapter of Second Corinthians, Paul shows us that these two issues of comfort and suffering are inseparably linked. The peace of God comes not because of an absence of trials, but because of His comfort in the midst of our suffering.

Paul fleshes all of this out a few chapters later in 2 Corinthians 4:8-9 when he says, "We are hard pressed on every side, but not crushed; perplexed, but not in despair; persecuted, but not abandoned; struck down, but not destroyed."

Done Got Run'd Over

*W*endy Bagwell, Southern gospel singer andcomedian, used to say, "Folks, what I'm 'bout to tell you is a fact with my hand up." This slogan usually preceded a story that might have appeared a little far-fetched. Well, this story is indeed "a fact, with my hand up". And the fact is I'm a little embarrassed that after one book and numerous newspaper and magazine articles, this is the first time it's made it to print. Folks, I'm 'bout to tell ya'll about the time I ran over myself with my own wheelchair.

Back in my college days, I was pretty rough on my power wheelchair. It wasn't on purpose or anything. It's just a fact of life. Just think about it. The average American has, what, eight to ten pair of shoes? And they wear different shoes depending on the specific occasion. I ain't got but one wheelchair. So, whether I was going to class, church, out with friends, hunting in the woods, or whatever, that was the chair I was going in. It went everywhere, through everything, and, just like everyday shoes, got a little roughed up.

Now, my best good friend, Justin Peters (aka Brother Bone), and I used to like to go out and throw the football around like college guys do. Despite his cerebral palsy, Justin was deadly accurate throwing the pigskin. My cerebral palsy has affected not only my legs, but my arms and hands as well. Bone would say, "Just go out. I'll put it in your spleen!" And he could. I'd put my wheelchair in rabbit mode, run a little ten to fifteen yard curl route, and he'd throw it to where a even little crippled man could catch it, sometimes "without even breaking stride". (One day ya'll will have to get me to tell you about the time we had the entire Mississippi State football team watching this little show…)

Problem was, between the football and my spleen was the joy-stick controller of my wheelchair. And that thing took a beating! In fact, it took such a beating that eventually, the joy-stick would not naturally return to a neutral position. See, a power wheelchair has magnetic breaks that automatically lock the rear tires when the controller is released. It's a safety feature. But my joy-stick had taken such a beating from our football games that this feature no longer worked. Now, I could turn it off, and it wouldn't move, but as long as the wheelchair was powered on, it would not sit still. It was like it was idled-up too high!

One Friday night, I was headed home from college for the weekend, and I decided to stop by and see my friend David Ezell. To get to David's home, you had to park in his grandmother's driveway, and then walk, or roll, around through the yard. It had been a particularly wet Spring, and without really thinking, I set off through the grass. Within moments, I found myself stuck in the mud, in no man's land between the two dwellings. No one knew I was coming, no one was expecting me, and no one knew where I was in particular. I'll tell ya where I was. I was stuck in the mud in my wheelchair in the dark with no one around to help. This was before cell phones mind you, and I was in a pickle!

I yelled and yelled for David, and after I decided no one was home, I decided that I was going to either have to figure out a way to help myself, or spend a long night outside. Despite my cerebral palsy, I can walk a little if I have my crutches or something else to hold on to. I turned in my seat, and pushed myself into a standing position facing the wheelchair. You must now realize as I did that trying to dislodge and set free the very thing that's keeping you upright is a dangerous business. Pushing my wheelchair backward with one hand, and guiding the controller in reverse with the other...I did just that...and fell face down in the mud.

Remember how I told you my wheelchair was idled up to high, well, I looked up just in time to see it heading right for me! I slid on my belly to left just quickly enough to avoid being hit in the face with the footrest. Now the wheelchair wasn't powerful enough to run completely over me, but I found myself pressed face-down in the mud, with the footrest on my back and the front tires grinding into my ribs.

I rolled with the momentum and turned on my back. Then I grabbed the footrest, tipped the wheelchair up and backward just enough to point it in a different direction, and with all my strength gave it a hard shove...and watched it roll down the hill without me. (I felt like a cowboy who'd been thrown by a stubborn horse that was now well on its way back to the barn.)

When my wheelchair slammed into David's trailer, he was jostled from his TV viewing slumber, and rescued me from the mire. I realize that self-deprecating humor is in my wheelhouse, but being pressed down in the mud by my own wheelchair gives me the perfect opportunity to talk about the Apostle Paul's treatise on suffering. 2 Corinthians 4:8a reads, "We are hard *pressed* on every side, but not crushed." No. By the grace of God, we get up, brush ourselves off, and get back in the game of life. Even if it's idled up a little too high.

Pumping Gas

*H*ave you ever been in an impossible situation? Have you ever been in a situation where there didn't seem to be any answer at all, much less a good one? As you can imagine, given my disability, I'm often confronted by "life's little quirks". Sometimes the quandaries can come over the most simple of things.

Take pumping gas, for example. Anytime Kelly and I travel together, and the vehicle we're in needs gas, we are in a pickle! To see why, first I'll have to explain the visual that the average stranger sees when I'm driving. The van Kelly and I drive has a remote control sliding door, a fold down wheelchair ramp, and a lock down system in the floorboard of the van that keeps the wheelchair from bouncing around like a pinball. After I lock my wheelchair in place, I transfer to the captain's chair in the van.

I drive using hand-controls. When I drive, I have my right hand on the spinner knob, attached to the steering wheel, and my left hand on the one lever that controls the gas and break. I'll pause here to say that if you meet me in traffic don't expect me to wave. I'm a little busy! Don't expect me to lose control of my vehicle and have a wreck just to placate your self-esteem issues! All that to say, if you are on the outside of the vehicle and you see me driving the vehicle, other than being perpetually rude for not waving, no one can distinguish me from any other able-bodied driver.

So why does this present such an enormous problem when we need to stop and get gas? Well, think about it. If Kelly gets out of the vehicle to pump gas, anyone driving by that situation will fold their arms and roll their eyes and say, at least to themselves, "Can you believe the nerve of that man? He's just sitting up in the comfort of his vehicle while his wife pumps the stinking gas!"

On the other hand, if I try to be the gentleman and get out of the vehicle to pump gas, anyone driving by that situation will cross their arms and roll their eyes and say, "Can you believe the nerve of that woman? She's just sitting up in the comfort and convenience of the vehicle while her crippled husband struggles to pump the gas!"

It's an impossible situation! After explaining this set of circumstances once, someone replied, "Well, why don't both of you get out?" Well, now what kind of idiot...! How silly would it be to have two people just camped out at the gas pump staring at one another.

It is a perplexing situation. Paul writes in 2 Cor. 4:8b that we are, "*perplexed*, but not in despair." Confused about some of the things going on in our lives? Well sure. Mentally desperate because we do not understand it all? Well no. Why? Because we hold the hand of the Author of Life, and He holds our future in His hands.

Persecuted…Sorta

*N*ehemiah 4:1-3 offers us an example of persecution. The author laments, "When Sanballat heard that we were rebuilding the wall, he became angry and was greatly incensed. He *ridiculed the Jews*, and in the presence of his associates and the army of Samaria, he said, 'What are *those feeble Jews* doing? Will they restore their wall? Will they offer sacrifices? Will they finish in a day? Can they bring the stones back to life from those heaps of rubble— burned as they are?' Tobiah the Ammonite, who was at his side, said, '*What they are building— even a fox climbing up on it would break down their wall of stones!*'"

Sadly, on some level, this is the worst type of ridicule the American Christian will ever know. Jesus said in John 15:20a, "Remember what I told you: 'A servant is not greater than his master.' If they *persecuted* me, they will *persecute* you also." Are you being persecuted for your faith? Probably not. Not to the point of anguish.

In my warped sense of humor, I can imagine the Apostle Paul starting a greeting card company specializing in a line of "Get Well Soon" cards. Maybe on the front cover one would read this quote from 2 Corinthians 11...

"I have worked much harder, been in prison more frequently, been flogged more severely, and been exposed to death again and again. Five times I received from the Jews the forty lashes minus one. Three times I was beaten with rods, once I was pelted with stones, three times I was shipwrecked, I spent a night and a day in the open sea, I have been constantly on the move. I have been in danger from rivers, in danger from bandits, in danger from my fellow Jews, in danger from Gentiles; in danger in the city, in danger in the country, in danger at sea; and in danger from false believers. I have labored and toiled and have often gone without sleep; I have known hunger and thirst and have often gone without food; I have been cold and naked."

Then you would open the card up, and on the inside it would read, "So...how ya been?" Have we been persecuted? For most of us the answer is no, not really. Not in light of what Paul went through. In view of Paul's tumultuous life, we should be reminded to keep things in *perspective*. And we should be reminded of God's *promise* that, even in *persecution*, we would never be abandoned.

The Ballad of Jake in Jasper

*T*his is where we find out that the Apostle Paul was indeed *not* Baptist. Notice in 2 Corinthians 4:8-9 he writes, "We are hard Pressed on every side, but not crushed; Perplexed, but not in despair; Persecuted, but not abandoned; Struck down, but not destroyed." Now which of those verbs just doesn't quite fit in with the others? See if Paul were a good Baptist, skilled at the art of alliteration, he would have used a fourth "P" word to finish out the sequence. Perhaps, instead of "struck down", he would have used the word "pummeled". And I can't think about the word pummeled without thinking about wrasslin'!

This particular wrasslin' story begins one Saturday in February that started like many other Saturdays. Kelly had some errands to run so she asked me to watch the kids for awhile. My five year old son, Will, and I had originally planned to go to a Professional Bull Riders event that night, but about middle of the morning I got a phone call that made that train jump the tracks in a hurry.

My good buddy, Rhett Barnett, called to tell me that World Wrestling Federation (aka WWE – World Wrestling Entertainment) legend Jake "The Snake" Roberts would be wrestling that night in Jasper, AL which is just about an hour from my home. I talked it over with Will. We decided that one redneck activity was just as good as another. Within a few hours we were off on another adventure, and I was taking a stroll down memory lane.

I grew up watching wrestling. I remember seeing Jake in the old Mid-South Wrestling promotion that later changed to the UWF, that later merged with the NWA, that later became WCW, that later merged with WWE. I could reminisce for several chapters, but I'll spare you all the details except for a few about Jake "The Snake". Jake wrestled the "Honky Tonk Man" in front of an announced crowd 93,173 at WrestleMania III at the Pontiac Silverdome in Michigan. And to overstate the obvious, that, my friends, is a far cry from the Swan High School Gymnasium in Jasper, Alabama.

Roberts was pushing sixty years old that night and suffering from a body that had been ravaged by the effects of drugs, alcohol, and even a cancerous tumor that was recently removed from behind his knee. But he still had a fire in his eyes, a smirk on his face, and, of course, the snake.

My buddies in college used to say, "There are two kinds of men in the world, those who watch wrestling... and those who lie and say they don't!" This statement may or may not be true. I am convinced of one truth, however. I once heard evangelist Rick Ousley say something like, "I believe that at any time of the day or night in the late eighties, you could turn on the television and always find two types of programming on cable TV. You could always find professional wrestling and religious programming. And I believe there were people watching both and asking the same question—'Is it real?'"

My question to you is the same. Is it real? Is the life you're living real? 2 Timothy 4:2 says, "Preach the word! Be ready in season and out of season. Convince, rebuke, exhort, with all longsuffering and teaching." 1 Peter 3:15 says, "But in your hearts set apart Christ as Lord. Always be prepared to give an answer to everyone who asks you to give the reason for the hope that you have. But do this with gentleness and respect."

Setting apart Christ as Lord is what it means to be a Christian. It means that we have surrendered our lives completely to Him. It means that we are no longer slaves to our selfishness and sins. We are servants of no one and nothing else but Christ alone. He is the reason for the hope that we have. And when you have that hope, just like those wrasslers, when you're pummeled, you won't be destroyed.

Will's Revelation

*A*s a parent, you always want what's best for your children. As a good parent, you must realize that what is best for your children is not always the thing that makes them happy. As a good Christian parent, I think it is imperative for us to allow our children to experience things that are uncomfortable, challenging, and maybe even painful in order for them to fully become all that God has called them to be.

Romans 5:3-5 reads, "...We also glory in our sufferings, because we know that suffering produces perseverance; perseverance, character; and character, hope. And hope does not put us to shame, because God's love has been poured out into our hearts through the Holy Spirit, who has been given to us."

All of this wisdom is cast into a different perspective in light of my disability. You see, I too want what's best for my children. And I must confess, I have, on occasion, wondered if a dad with a disability is the best kind of dad to have. I will never kick the soccer ball with them. I will never build them a tree-house. And there are countless scenarios where I could envision them being in peril, and me being physically helpless to do anything about it.

However, since well before I was able to articulate the thought, I have sensed that God was using my disability to help me know Him in ways that I would not have otherwise. My cerebral palsy brings new meaning to "when I am weak, then I am strong"(2 Cor. 12:10). Having a severe physical disability shines a new light on "not by works, so that no one can boast"(Eph 2:9). Being in a wheelchair for fifteen hours everyday puts a different perspective on "by the grace of God I am what I am"(1 Cor. 15:10). My disability has taught me a humility before God and a dependence upon God that I doubt I would have experienced were it not for this circumstance.

Therefore, because of my limited insight and understanding, do I wish for the ability to physically give my children every opportunity and advantage? Sure. Do I also believe in the infinite goodness and sovereignty of God? You bet. So maybe, just maybe, I'm not the only one learning lessons from this condition. Maybe this disability not only helps me to know God, but also to make Him known.

This lesson was never so clear to me as when Will and I were loading into the van once, and seeing me struggle to transfer from my wheelchair to the driver's seat, Will said, "Dad, I wish you could walk." I just said the first thing that came to mind. "Yeah, and sometimes, son, I do to. But you know, I think that when people see my legs don't work, and they see how much I love God anyway, that helps them love God a little more." And that kid just got the biggest smile on his little face and said, "Yeah, Dad. Yeah."

I'm reminded of this little conversation over and over again during the trying circumstances of my life and reflect on the words the Apostle Paul used to close the fourth chapter of Second Corinthians. "For we who are alive are always being given over to *death* for Jesus' sake, so that His *life* may also be revealed in our mortal body. So then, *death is at work in us, but life is at work in you.* Therefore we do not lose heart. *Though outwardly we are wasting away, yet inwardly we are being renewed day by day.* For our light and momentary troubles are achieving for us an eternal glory that far outweighs them all."

A Little Social Commentary

I'll Just Keep This To Myself

*T*here is an intersection not far from my
home that confuses me every time I approach it.
It is not necessarily unique. In fact, you probably
have one similar near you. Maybe it's just my
simple-mindedness, but this thing is just baffling
to me.

The crossroads of which I speak is the
intersection of Highway 31 and Interstate 65 in
Vestavia, Alabama, a suburb of Birmingham.
Every time I'm traveling west on 31 and need to
take I-65 south I really have to take some deep
cleansing breaths to make sure I make the correct
decisions.

Now, here's the first lesson. I've been
taught that roadways with odd numbers run north
and south, and that those with even numbers run
east and west. And I realize that, if that's true,
then I could not possibly travel west on

Highway 31. However, two counterpoints come to mind. First, if you are traveling down a stretch of road in the afternoon and the sun is in your eyes, you're headed west...no matter what the signs say. Secondly, if I'm traveling on 31-South and then exit onto 65-South, why is it that I'm headed in an entirely new direction?

But I digress. That isn't even my primary quandary. The point is that if I'm headed west, and need to go south, then I should turn left, right? (I mean "correct?") Not at this intersection! No, here in bizarro world, motorist facing the setting sun turn left to go north, and right to travel south.

Now my next day of work with the Department of Transportation will be my first. But I can't for the life of me figure out why they constructed this ramp system in this manner. Maybe the average driver doesn't have the keenly developed sense of direction that I do. Maybe it never enters their mind. But virtually every time I come near this interchange I have to fight my natural inclinations in order to get to where I need to go.

Such is the spiritual world we are living in today. There's a prevailing worldview, even among some churches, that a person can become a Christian without it affecting their everyday life. In other words, "I can 'pray the sinners prayer, and ask Jesus into my heart', get saved, get my 'Get Out of Hell Free' card, get my 'Fire Insurance Policy'…but this whole 'Christianity thing' doesn't have to take over my life. I'll just do whatever *feels* right. And I really don't need the Holy Bible's instruction or direction." Well, dear friends, that's just not what Scripture teaches:

"Grace and peace be yours in abundance through the knowledge of God and of Jesus our Lord. His divine power has given us *everything* we need for *life* and godliness through our *knowledge* of him who called us by his own glory and goodness. Through these he has given us his very great and precious promises, so that through them you may participate in the divine nature and escape the corruption in the world caused by evil desires" – 2 Peter 1:2-4

"Let the word of Christ richly dwell within you, with *all* wisdom, teaching and admonishing one another with psalms and hymns and spiritual songs, singing with thankfulness in your hearts to God. *Whatever* you do in word or deed, do *all* in the name of the Lord Jesus, giving thanks through Him to God the Father." - Colossians 3:16-17

" Therefore I urge you, brethren, by the mercies of God, to present your bodies a living and holy sacrifice, acceptable to God, which is your spiritual service of worship. And do not be conformed to this world, but *be transformed by the renewing of your mind*, so that you may prove what the will of God is, that which is good and acceptable and perfect." - Romans 12:1-2

"But have *nothing* to do with worldly fables fit only for old women. On the other hand, discipline yourself for the purpose of godliness; for bodily discipline is only of little profit, but godliness is profitable for *all* things, since it holds promise for the present life and also for the life to come. *It is a trustworthy statement deserving full acceptance.*" - 1 Timothy 4:7-9

"*All* Scripture is inspired by God and profitable for *teaching*, for reproof, for *correction*, for *training* in righteousness; so that the man of God may be adequate, equipped for *every* good work." - 2 Timothy 3:15-17

Country music singer Aaron Tippin crooned, "You've got to stand for something or you'll fall for anything." And it's true. If we don't use the Bible as the compass for every aspect of our lives, we are in danger of losing our way. So let us dedicate ourselves to being people of the Book. Let us read, and study, and learn, and apply the Holy Scriptures to our lives. "Then we will no longer be infants, tossed back and forth by the waves, and blown here and there by every wind of teaching and by the cunning and craftiness of people in their deceitful scheming." (Eph. 4:14)

The Virtues of...Soccer?

*W*hen he was three years old Will started playing soccer in our city league, the Moody Soccer Club. (I will pause immediately here to say that, while I never was and probably never will be a true soccer fan, I do not think that it is part of some covert Communist plot to overthrow America.) Will loves playing soccer, but, bless his heart, he's got some challenges to overcome.

First of all, because of when his birthday falls, he is often the youngest player on the field. Secondly, he is genetically disadvantaged. Kelly and I both are in the five foot-five inch range; so he's vertically challenged, and he gets it honestly. When Will started playing, his legs were so short that my dad said that Will would "do better to lay down and roll" in order to get to the ball faster. Not only is he the youngest and the smallest, he's also quite distracted at times with some other things he's got going on in his mind.

Will wants to be superhero when he grows up. So for practice, he pretends to be one virtually every waking moment of his life right now. Usually, first thing in the morning, he announces who he's going to "be" for the day. The current list of usual suspects would include: Superman, Spiderman, The Hulk, Wolverine, a Power Ranger, Captain America and maybe the occasional Ninja Turtle. You've heard of an actor "becoming the part"? Well, let's just say that Will takes his "roles" very seriously. And don't you dare think he's above wearing a full costume to church or the store or wherever we happen to be headed!

Now the parents and coaches at soccer practice are more than willing to play along with Will's adopted persona. In fact, their first question upon his arrival is not "How are you today?", but "Who are you today?" And of course Will smiles, and tells them, and then that's what everyone calls him for the rest of his time on the field that day. But telling a three year old, who wants to be a superhero, "Good work today, Batman", is like pouring gasoline on a fire!

As much as Will loves the attention, this is, as I mentioned, a distraction if the intended result while on the field is to actually be playing soccer! Trying to turn this into an advantage, I told Will before one game, "Hey, Wolverine. Pretend the soccer ball is the bad guys, and the goal is the jail. Then you can kick those evil doers all the way to the gray bar motel!" Do you think he was fired up? Man, yeah! Unfortunately, he spent most of the game talking on his pretend wrist-mounted communication device calling for back-up!

Kelly and I were frustrated. On the one hand, he's only three years old, and if the intent of this whole experience is to have fun, then Will has certainly excelled in that effort. On the other hand, we paid good money for soccer balls, jerseys, shin guards and cleats. Not to mention the registration fee for the league. If all he wants to do is be a superhero, he can do that in the backyard…for free! So you don't want to be "that parent" that expects way too much of their child at such a young age, but you don't want to raise a child that never takes anything seriously either.

After both and Kelly and I attempted repeated efforts of briefly mentioning our disapproval with his performance, both during and after games and practices, I decided Will and I needed to have a talk. We were unloading from the mini-van before practice. I helped him out of his car seat and was trying to explain what we expected, and he was obviously not paying attention. I gave him a little pop on the bottom.

(Calm down. Calm down! I didn't break his pelvis or anything. But I did make sure he knew this was a serious conversation.) Guess what. It only took one more of those "conversations" for Will's soccer experience to change drastically.

In fact, he took on a whole new persona. At the next game, when someone asked him who he was, he said, "Will Fisher...soccer player!" And he played like it! He ran to the ball, he kicked the ball, no "flying" in circles, no calling for back-up. He even scored his first goal! I could not have been prouder if he had been playing football for Mississippi State University and they had just won the national championship! ("Yeah, right! Like that's ever gonna happen!" Hey, if you'd seen Will's first six weeks of Spring soccer, you would have said the odds of either happening were pretty much identical!)

Hebrews 12:7-11 reveals what I feel are some important points on this topic. "Endure hardship as *discipline*; God is treating you as his children. For what children are not *disciplined* by their father? If you are not *disciplined*—and everyone undergoes *discipline* —then you are not legitimate, not true sons and daughters at all. Moreover, we have all had human fathers who *disciplined* us and we respected them for it. How much more should we submit to the Father of spirits and live! They *disciplined* us for a little while as they thought best; but God *disciplines* us for our good, in order that we may share in his holiness. No *discipline* seems pleasant at the time, but painful. Later on, however, it produces a harvest of righteousness and peace for those who have been trained by it."

My discipline of Will did not change Will physically. He's still "genetically disadvantaged". But it changed his attitude. And, don't get me wrong, his change of attitude didn't make him magically run circles around the other players. But he kept trying, and kept trying. And he was in the right place, at the right time, and he scored! I think God calls us to a similar life; accept discipline, keep plodding, ...score! Hey, maybe soccer's not so bad after all.

Saved!...From What?

*O*ver the past few years, I've become increasingly burdened by the fact that I have a Biblical mandate to be the spiritual leader of my household and the primary faith teacher to my children. I have also been challenged by leaders in my church and other sources to not only feel convicted about these duties, but to actually take steps to carry out my obligations. In accordance with all of this, and with Easter rapidly approaching one year, I decided to have a theological discussion with my son.

Now having any conversation with a preschooler, much less a spiritual one, is challenging to say the least. But, it is never too early to start talking to your children about God. Will loves for me to wrestle with him, and it was during one of these bouts that I felt I had his undivided attention. In between rounds, while we were resting, I thought this might be a great time for some "God moments". During our conversation I said, "Did you know that Jesus came to save and rescue us? Will's reply, "Was he a fireman, or a Power Ranger?"

That question may make you giggle, but I think it involves an evangelical angle we must consider. I believe that Will, at that age, did not fully understand the concept of sinning against a Holy God. When he thought about being "rescued" or "saved", in his mind it had to be from burning buildings or evil Ngylock warriors.

Why is this relevant? Well, I think many times we become entrenched in using "Christianeese". That is, terminology that Christians know and understand, but that unbelievers might be unfamiliar. During the "big" religious holidays of Christmas and Easter someone might ask why we celebrate. Our response might be, "Because Jesus came to save us." Their appropriate question then might be, "From what?"

The logical response then is, "From our sins." There it is…the "S" word. It's not the first time you've seen that word, is it? I mean it only appears in the Bible about 500 times! (That's not an exaggeration for emphasis. I looked it up!) But more important than the number of times it appears, is the depth and breadth to which human history has been impacted by that little three letter word.

Think about it. Hypothetically, if Eve had never been tempted, then the one fruit fiasco would never have occurred, this plague upon mankind would never have been perpetuated, and we would all still be living in the paradise of Eden. But she was, and it did, and it is, and we're not! I know it's not popular to talk about, but it is our sin that separates us from Holy God.

So talk about it we must! It is essential to salvation, to evangelism, to the faith. Think about it. If you tell someone to wear a life-preserver because it will make them feel good, or help them with their finances, or their relationships, they will be reluctant to put it on, and fast to remove it if there are not immediate positive results. But explain to them that they are about to *drown*, and then a certain urgency takes hold.

This, by the way, is the difference between Christianity and every other major world religion. Every other faith group says, "Follow us, and we will teach you how to swim." The Bible on the contrary says in Galatians 2:16, "Know that a person is not justified by the works of the law, but by faith in Jesus Christ. So we, too, have put our faith in Christ Jesus that we may be justified by faith in Christ and not by the works of the law, because by the works of the law no one will be justified."

We all stand in need of rescue. Not by a fireman. Not by a Power Ranger. But by the Lord, Jesus Christ. No wonder they call Him the Savior!

The Tradeoff

*T*here is a governing principle in economics called the "Equality-Efficiency Tradeoff." It basically states that a society's efforts to make the incomes of its citizens more equal, will inherit the adverse effects of a decrease in efficiency (or productivity) from those citizens. Why would a society need to make an effort to make the incomes of its citizens more equal? Well, because they are unequal (or inequal) to begin with, of course. Why are they unequal? That is a great place to begin our discussion.

In a predominantly free-market capitalistic economic system, such as the United States has, the major reason incomes are unequal is that this system rewards its citizens based on their abilities. The pre-amble to our Constitution states that "all men are created equal", but equal does not mean same. We all have different abilities; things we do well, and things we don't do so well. Our society rewards its citizens based on the satisfaction that buyers receive (economist call this "utility") when they pay to enjoy our abilities.

Allow me a personal illustration. Let me tell you about two people that I admire. The first is my wife. Kelly works for an organization called "Pre-School Partners", affectionately referred to as PSP. It's a non-profit organization that targets three and four year old children from inner-city Birmingham. Many of these kids are from low-income, single parent homes, and this program is designed to prepare them for kindergarten. The program is extremely affordable, yet the parents are required to take classes also, in things like time management, anger management, and money management. Sound like a program that is making a positive impact on the demographic it was intended to serve? Statistics say so. Five years after leaving the program, PSP kids have higher grades and better attendance records than their counterparts who did not complete the program. Do you think Kelly's work makes a valuable contribution to society? I think so.

The second person I'll tell you about is a guy named Peyton Manning. You may have heard of him. He's won the NFL's Most Valuable Player Award an unprecedented four times. His last contract to play the game of football was reportedly in the neighborhood of $69 million over three years. Let me pause here to say that Kelly makes significantly less than that. Why? Is it because her contributions to the well being and functionality of our society are significantly less than Peyton's? No. It's because no one has ever lined up to pay $150 each to watch Kelly teach letters and numbers.

Now we can argue that society *should* value its teachers (and police officers, and paramedics, and firefighters, and so on) over its athletes, but do we? I once heard someone say, "You show me your calendar and your bank statement, and I'll show you what's important to you." The things we spend time and money on are the things that are truly important to us. And our society values entertainment. Many people are willing to pay their hard earned money to watch Peyton execute his abilities, where they are not willing to do so for Kelly's.

Is this fair? I have three thoughts in response to this question.

First, life is not fair. Anyone who tells you otherwise is selling something. We are imperfect people, living in an imperfect world, and because of that, life will never be perfect.

Second, and this is the principle most fail to comprehend, Peyton's ability to make $23 million a year, doesn't decrease Kelly's opportunity to make that much. Wealth is not like a great big pie that, when divided, means that if you get a bigger slice, I, by definition, get a smaller one. Wealth creates more wealth. Peyton making big money means that someone has to build a big stadium for him to play in, and someone has to make jerseys with his name and number on them (for him and thousands of fans), and someone has to make hot dogs that sell for $15 at that stadium on the days he's wearing that jersey, and executing his abilities.

Third, and lastly, I would ask anyone who asks "Is this system fair?" to explain to me another system that has historically set a precedent for greater fairness.

Now, if we have a system that creates so much inequality, (and we do) and we begin to value equality (which we have), what steps could we take to ensure more income equality? Two things could accomplish this; a progressive tax structure and transfer payments.

A progressive tax is taxing a higher fraction of a higher income. A progressive tax bracket structure takes more money away from rich people, which by definition makes them poorer. Transfer payments then take some of that money and give it to poorer people (in the form of Social Security, and food stamps, and earned income tax credits), which by definition makes them richer. That's how you bring about greater income equality.

The negative, unintended side- affect to these practices is that it gives both groups less incentive to be productive. In fact, it gives both groups more incentive to be less productive; less efficient. As a rich person, why would you work hard to make more, if the reward would be that more would be taken? As a poor person, why would you work hard to make more, if the reward would be that less would be given? (Incidentally, if you do not believe that most people are driven by individual ambition and incentive, I would love for you to introduce to me these angels among us.)

Allow me a second personal illustration. Since I was born with cerebral palsy, according the laws of our land, I am fully qualified to receive a Supplemental Security Income (SSI) check (commonly known as "Disability") from the federal government each month. However, at some point I decided that I wanted more out of life. In high school I studied and made good grades and did well on the ACT. I earned scholarships to college, and studied, and made good grades. I am now a gainfully employed, productive, tax-paying member of society. I teach economics at a college.

One day, during a break between semesters, I decided to go fishing. While fishing off the dock, I noticed a car pull into the parking lot. The driver, a guy who appeared to be about my age, hopped out of the car and seemed to have no trouble carrying a large bag of charcoal. He made another trip from his car to the picnic table, this time carrying coolers and other odds and ends. On his third trip, he gathered his tackle box and rod and reels, and headed my way.

We chatted for awhile, while we fished, as fisherman often do. During the course of our conversation I asked, "What do you do?" He said, "Oh, I, uh…draw a disability check." Now I'm as friendly as the next guy, and we continued to talk and fish for quite some time.

But sometime later I realized something. Every day the alarm goes off, I struggle with the challenge to get out of bed. I struggle with the challenge of getting dressed. I struggle with the challenge of getting into my vehicle, sometimes with the added challenge of buckling my children into their car-seats when I'm in charge of day care. On the job, I work to adequately perform the required duties of my position.

And I do all of this so that (among other things), on occasion I may enjoy some leisure time – like fishing. I also realized that, meanwhile I am receiving another reward for my diligence, good choices, and hard work. I get to pay taxes! And some of those taxes go to pay the disability check of my fishing buddy!

Now let me ask you a question: If someone had explained to me during my formative years that this is the way things would be, do you think it would have provided me any incentive to press forward? Do you think, if someone had told me that this is the way the world works, that I would have been more motivated to set goals or try to achieve more in life? I don't. In fact, I might have been persuaded to take advantage of the hand-outs being offered. It would have certainly been easier.

This is the "Equality-Efficiency Tradeoff." And it gives both groups less incentive. It gives "rich people" less incentive, for they know the more they work, the more will be taken. It gives "poor people" less incentive, for they know the less they work, the more will be given.

In 1990, in his book "Free to Choose", Milton Friedman said, "A society that puts equality before freedom will get neither." It seems that over twenty years later, we still haven't heeded this warning. It shouldn't surprise us. Some two thousand years ago, the Apostle Paul's words were, "For even when we were with you, *this we commanded you, that if any would not work, neither should he eat*. For we hear that there are some which walk among you disorderly, working not at all, but are busybodies." (2 Thessolonians 3:10-11, KJV)

We haven't obeyed this command either. And many years before that, King Solomon wrote in Proverbs 24:3-34, "A little sleep, a little slumber, a little folding of the hands to rest—and poverty will come on you like a thief and scarcity like an armed man."

Tremors

I realize that for those who know me, and understand a little bit about my disability, the title of this chapter might be a bit misleading. You might think that because my cerebral palsy causes spasticity, that the title might be referring to the trembling that occurs in my muscles from time to time. No, the title is from the *movie* "Tremors".

"Tremors" is a movie that some would call a "cult classic". (That is not to say that this movie is of the occult. The acting is horrible, the plot line flimsy, and the special effects are bad. But I don't think it's 'of the Devil".) A "cult classic" is, in my opinion, a lesser known movie whose fans are truly fanatical. They've seen the movie dozens upon dozens of times, can quote from memory entire dialogue sequences, and probably have dressed up at least once on Halloween as one of its characters.

Such is the case with "Tremors". It's a low budget flick about, stay with me here, people in a small isolated town defending themselves against underground alien monsters. It stars, and I use that term loosely, Fred Ward and a young Kevin Bacon. Let me end all debate and controversy here by stating, "I *love* this movie!"

Allow me here a little stroll down amnesia lane to explain how this little movie came to reside permanently in the top twenty of my "all-time favorites" list. I grew up in a very rural area. Some people might even call it the boonies. To say that cable television was slow in coming to our community (and I use that term loosely as well) would be an understatement. (Maybe they didn't have enough line to run out that far. I don't know.) We didn't go to movies as a family when I was growing up. (You'll have to ask Big Bill and Momma Fay about that.) But I developed a friendship with the new kid in school my eighth grade year named Jeremy. And Jeremy had *two* VCRs.

Now, if it weren't prohibited under federal law, Jeremy might have made copies of movies he rented. And if he had made copies he might have loaned them out to his friends. And if he had made and loaned, one of the movies might have been "Tremors". And if Tremors were one of those movies, he might have made me a copy, and my brother and I might have watched it. And being starved for entertainment such as we were in rural Mississippi in the summertime with no cable or satellite TV, we might have watched it about a hundred times.

In one scene from the movie, Fred Ward and Kevin Bacon's characters find themselves on top of a large boulder surrounded by these underground alien monsters. The monsters can't penetrate the rock, so our heroes are safe for the moment, but as time goes on, they realize they will die of thirst or hunger before the monsters simply leave of their own accord. The conversation on top of the boulder goes something like this:

> Fred: "What we need is a *plan*."
>
> Kevin: "I say we just run for it!"
>
> Fred: "Running's not a plan. Running is what you do when a *plan* fails!"

May I ask you a question? Are you *planning* to go to church this Sunday? If so, do you have *a plan*? Or are you just running? How many of us put as much energy and effort into getting our kids and ourselves ready to go to His house on His day as we do into getting to work and school on time on Monday? Do you set an alarm? Did you gas up the day before so you won't have to stop on the way? Will you leave fifteen minutes early...just in case.

I think, for many of us, one of our problems is that we think getting to church on time will just happen. We think that since we don't have to be at church as early as we do work and school, there'll be plenty of time to get everything done. This just isn't true. I don't know about your house, but our house can be anything but peaceful on a Sunday morning. And the Devil will jump on you with both feet to give you any excuse not to go to worship. Or, better yet, he'll make you so frazzled by the time you get there, that you're not able to worship.

Hebrews 10:24-27 reads, "And let us consider how we may spur one another on toward love and good deeds. *Let us not give up meeting together, as some are in the habit of doing,* but let us encourage one another—and all the more as you see the Day approaching. *If we deliberately keep on sinning after we have received the knowledge of the truth*, no sacrifice for sins is left, but *only a fearful expectation of judgment* and of raging fire that will consume the enemies of God."

Now, hear me out. I, for the most part, am not naturally bent toward legalism. I don't think it is necessarily a sin to miss church once in awhile. In fact, I think there are some legitimate reasons for missing church. On the other hand, I've heard people say, "God doesn't call roll on Sunday mornings." Well, that might be, but I also don't believe we should abuse the precious gifts of grace and mercy that He so generously bestows upon us.

So, what to make of this thing we call "going to church"? Do we attend regularly? Is attending half of the time to be considered "regular"? Is being fifteen to twenty minutes late when we do attend really giving our best in an effort to serve a risen Savior? How do we attempt to correct these issues? Well, we must have a plan! Why? Because, "Proper planning prevents potential problems and poor performance."

Will there be Sundays that are absolutely crazy at your house? Sure. Will there be times when everything that can go wrong on Sunday mornings will indeed go wrong? You bet. Are there going to be times where "the best laid plans" have indeed gone awry, and the only option you have left is just to run? Of course. But remember: Running's not a plan! Running is what you do when a plan fails!

Thoughts from Father Harbaugh

*T*he 2013 Super Bowl (that would be Super Bowl XLVII, for those who speak Roman numeral) was nicknamed the "Har-Bowl". Why? Because for the first time in NFL history, two brothers, John and Jim Harbaugh, faced off as the head coaches of their respective teams. There were other intriguing story lines in the game. Ray Lewis, the linebacker for the Baltimore Ravens once accused of murder, had announced his retirement and was playing in his final game. Colin Kaepernick, the quarterback for the San Francisco 49ers with a cannon for an arm and video game type moves, had led the '9ers to a Super Bowl in just his second year out of college. But it was the "brother versus brother" match-up that compelled many to tune in.

I heard a radio interview with Jack Harbaugh, the father of Jim and John, just hours before the game. There were the usual questions: "Are you nervous?" "How's your wife, Jackie, holding up through all of this?" "How proud are you of your sons?" But the question and answer that really got me to thinking was near the end of the interview. The reporter asked, "How will you spend that three and a half hours during the game?" (How could the reporter have known that there would be a blackout in half of the New Orleans Superdome that would halt play for thirty-five minutes?) Jack's response, "Well, there's no emotion. 'Cause you have to know that if something good happens for one, it's bad for the other. And vice versa."

Wow. What an incredibly difficult position. Now, as a father, I can kind of get my mind around my children competing against one another. But as a football fan...now you've sucked all of the fun out of the game. Those of you who are football fans know that the games are most fun when you become emotionally invested. It's thrilling when "your team" wins, even if you have no logical, financial or geographical connection to the team. That's why they call us "fans"; because we're fanatical about "our team". What an impossible situation to be faced with. When two things you love face off, it's a "zero sum game". Somebody wins. Somebody loses. But there's no emotion.

The Bible has a bit to say about this. In Matthew 6:24 Jesus said, "No one can serve two masters. Either you will hate the one and love the other, or you will be devoted to the one and despise the other. You cannot serve both God and money." Now, your "other love" may not be cash. It may be your comfort, or your convenience or your children. It may be your reputation, or your relationships, or even your religion. But if there's anything in our life that impacts any segment of our life more than following the will of God, it's an idol.

The Old Testament tells us time and again about the children of Israel getting caught up in idol worship. 2 Kings 17:8-12 is one such passage:

(They) followed the practices of the nations the Lord had driven out before them, as well as the practices that the kings of Israel had introduced. The Israelites secretly did things against the Lord their God that were not right. From watchtower to fortified city they built themselves high places in all their towns. They set up sacred stones and Asherah poles on every high hill and under every spreading tree. At every high place they burned incense, as the nations whom the Lord had driven out before them had done. *They did wicked things that aroused the Lord's anger. They worshiped idols,*

though the Lord had said, "You shall not do this."

There is so much that could be unpacked from these verses. I think the knee jerk reaction for many Christians goes something like, "Whew! Glad I don't have any idols in my life. I mean I don't have any Asherah poles or sacred stones, and I don't burn incense to Baal. Check that off the list. I'm in the clear." But notice that this passage begins by saying they "followed the practices of the nations". Do you know what that means? It means that they were just doing what everybody else was doing!

You see, an idol doesn't have to be illegal (like a drug addiction or sacrificing your children in a fire). It doesn't have to be culturally unacceptable (like abandoning your wife). It may even be accepted, uplifted and applauded by your circle of Christian friends. But if there is anything, yes anything, that causes you to hesitate about following the will of God, it could very well be an idol.

Christian George writes in the Gospel Project, "The question is not if we are worshiping; the question is what we are worshiping. Any attention we give to idols is attention we deflect from God...robbing God of the glory that is rightfully His. The God of the Bible describes Himself as 'jealous'. God does not play second fiddle. He never has and He never will." God is not jealous of us or for us. He is jealous for Himself. That is because He alone is true, and perfect, and holy, and sovereign, he is worthy of all worship and will indeed be glorified!

In 1 Kings 18:21, the prophet Elijah asked the children of Israel, "How long will you hesitate between two opinions?" (HCSB) How many of us have halted in our walk with the Lord? How many do not know which way to turn? We have a longing to serve God, but the allure of worldly things has taken precedence in our lives. Pray today, if you dare, that God would reveal the idols in your life...and pray for the resolve to destroy them.

A Closer

Look

At

Ephesians 2

Introduction: Just to Position

*T*he second chapter of the New Testament book of Ephesians begins with what theologians would call a "Pauline Juxtaposition". I know. I know. You're saying, "Justin, you're from Conehatta, Mississippi. You ain't supposed to be usin' them four dollar words that can't nobody understand!" Well, relax. Calm down. I'm gonna 'splain 'em to ya.

First of all, the writing is "Pauline" in nature because the Apostle Paul wrote the Book of Ephesians. That and approximately one third of the entire New Testament. Paul, you know the one first called Saul, who held the coats and watched with glee as Stephen was martyred (Acts 7:58). Paul, you know the one, who came face to face with the risen Savior on the Damascus Road and was not only changed in name, but in heart and deed and life, radically and forevermore. It

120

was Paul who gave us the greatest treatise ever written on love (1 Cor. 13). And it was Paul who called himself the chief of sinners (1 Tim. 1:15) and the least of saints (Eph. 3:8).

So, here's the deal, if you took every story, blog, newspaper article, magazine article and book I've written and compared them, you would notice a similar style, phraseology, tone, even similar themes. It's the same way with Brother Paul. All of his letters included for us in the Holy Bible, all thirteen of them, have identifiers that make them unquestionably "Pauline".

By the way, when it comes to the Word of God that we call the Bible, I do not believe in the "mechanical dictation" theory. ("There you go again using them big words.") I do not believe that God turned the authors into "robots" and caused them to write His words. I believe in "verbal plenary". (Last one. I promise.) That is to say that God used everything in the authors' lives from the region they lived, the language they were taught, their education, and their struggles to uniquely capture the exactness and the essence of God's Word for us. And so the Holy Spirit of God used the free-will of these men to work in perfect harmony, concert, and compatibility with the sovereignty of God.

So Ephesians is uniquely Pauline, and Paul uses juxtaposition. Juxtaposition is when you put two things side by side for comparison. Maybe I'm not supposed to, but I really like that big word. In fact, I originally titled my first book, "Juxtapositions: Just to Position Justin's Position". It got shot down by friends and family alike, and "Can't Even Walk" was a much better fit. But the original title was completely accurate. In that book, and this one, I put my real life happenings side by side with Scripture for comparison.

So where's the juxtaposition in Ephesians, chapter two. Well, it actually comes in the transition between chapters one and two. Notice in Ephesians 1:18 and following, Paul begins this prayer for the saints in Ephesus that the, "eyes of your heart may be enlightened in order that you may know" (three very important things) "the *hope* to which he has called you, the *riches* of his glorious inheritance in his holy people, and his incomparably great *power* for us who believe."

Then Paul goes to great lengths to explain to them exactly what that power, that is available to them and us, is capable of. "That power is the same as the mighty strength he exerted when he raised Christ from the dead and seated him at his right hand in the heavenly realms, far above *all* rule and authority, power and dominion, and *every* name that is invoked, not only in the present age but also in the one to come. And God placed *all* things under his feet and appointed him to be head over *everything* for the church, which is his body, the fullness of him who fills *everything* in *every* way."

Paul begins by reminding us that God has raised Christ from the dead. And if Christ is risen from the dead, then he is alive! That alone is enough to praise Him for! If that don't light your fire, then your wood must be wet! But Paul doesn't stop there! He goes on to tell us that, because God has seated Jesus at His right hand, Christ is above some particular things: rule, authority, power, dominion and every name that is, or ever will be, invoked. And then, in case we didn't catch it the first time, Paul says the same thing in the opposite way. After telling us what Christ is above, he then tells us what is below Christ: all things and everything!

If I may be so bold as to summarize, "Jesus is IT!" He is alive, and seated on His throne, and ruling, and reigning over everything in every way. Jesus is alive. Not even the heathens call him "The late Jesus of Nazareth".

Then comes the juxtaposition, the comparison, in Ephesians 2:1, ""As for you, you were *dead...*"

Dead Man Walking

*T*he comparison is striking, and the implications are obvious. Jesus is IT…and you are NOT! "As for you, you were dead in your transgressions and sins…"(Eph. 2:1). Let me tell you a story about being dead. It comes from a psychiatrist dealing with the criminally insane at a maximum security prison. He had a patient who believed himself dead. There was no reasoning with the man. Never mind that he was walking among the living. In his mind he truly believed he was no longer alive.

The doctor, in an effort to counsel the inmate, asked, "Do dead people bleed?" The inmate assured his counselor that dead people certainly did not bleed. Then the doctor asked if it would be okay if a nurse came in and pricked the patient's finger to be sure that he was dead. "After all," the doctor said, "We can't have a dead person walking around scaring other inmates who are already mentally unstable." The dead man consented. The nurse came in, his finger was pricked, and amazingly a crimson liquid oozed from the small opening. Starring incredulously at his finger the inmate announced, "Well, I'll be! Dead people DO bleed!"

Do you know what is worse than being alive, yet thinking you are dead? It is thinking you are alive, yet in truth being dead. Ever since the fall of man in the Garden of Eden, the human race has found itself dead and dying. And in case you think the writer is not talking to you, Paul continues in verse three by saying "all of us". But the prevailing world view of our culture disagrees. The common thought is, "I'm OK. You're OK. And at the end of the day, everything's going to be OK. Hey, hey!" Even those of us who claim the truth of Scripture often have a distorted or skewed concept of this "deadness".

This reminds me of a scene in the movie "The Princess Bride", a spoof on the traditional fairy tale. When the evil prince kills the humble farm boy, Billy Crystal's character, Miracle Max, is about to ask a question of the corpse. A bystander declares, "He's dead. He can't talk." Max's response: "Look who knows so much, heh? Well, it just so happens that your friend here is only *mostly* dead. There's a big difference between *mostly* dead and all dead. And mostly dead is slightly alive."

So it is with most people. Even if we believe we're dead, deep down we believe we're only mostly dead. We believe that there is part of our being that is alive and well and good. And that if we try hard enough, we can lift ourselves up by our bootstraps, and elevate ourselves to a higher moral standard. Dear friends it simply is not so. We are not sick people in need of a doctor. We are dead people in need of a Savior!

So just to make sure none of us thinks we're "slightly alive", Paul contrasts our "deadness" with Christ's "aliveness". Christ is ruler over everything, and we are but followers. We follow the ways of this world, and we follow the cravings of our flesh and its desires.

Disobedient? Who me?

I am a Mississippi author and proud of it. I love to list the long line of award winning, distinguished writers from my home state. Folks like Tennessee Williams, William Faulkner, Eudora Welty, and John Grisham are just the tip of the iceberg when it comes to the talent produced by what I've nicknamed "The Storytelling State." I am quick to admit, however, that I am not nearly as talented as these folks. In fact, I'm not really creative at all. I don't anguish over developing the perfect character, setting, tone, mood, conflict or plot-line.

Over the course of writing two books, I've realized that my gifting from God is to take every-day events and pair them with Scripture to teach life application. "I don't write the news, I just report it!" Sometimes an event happens and afterward I discover a Bible verse that relates. Other times, I read Scripture and the Word of God reminds me of a particular occurrence.

Ephesians 2:1-2 reads, "And you were dead in the trespasses and sins in which you once walked, following the course of this world, following the prince of the power of the air, the spirit that is now at work in the *sons of disobedience*." (ESV) I wish I had a great example here of a funny story about a particular time that our children were being disobedient. But I don't because I guess Kelly and I are raising perfect children. If you'll buy that, I've got some ocean-front property in Arizona for sale that I'd like for you to make me an offer on.

Are you kidding me? I could fill volumes with just stories of my children being bad. I tell folks that if they ever doubted the existence of original sin, they just need to come hang out at my house for a little while. I know that in

2 Corinthians 11:14 when Paul tells us that "Satan himself masquerades as an angel of light," he wasn't specifically talking about my children...but sometimes I wonder.

"No, little girl, you can't wear a sundress when it's nineteen degrees outside!" "No, your brother did not make this mess, because he's still at school and has been all day." "Son, why have you left your shoes *and underwear* outside in the rain?" Who do you think taught my children to lie, to make mischief, to disobey? The answer, no one. We, all of us, are inherently evil. We are all sons and daughters of disobedience. And because of that we deserve God's wrath...

This Is Where It Gets Good

*W*e've all got that movie. You know, the one you absolutely love, but no one else has seen. And then the time finally comes that you're all hanging out, with nothing really going on, and you say, "Hey, let's watch this." Your friends consent, but about twenty minutes in, they're confused, or bored, and ready to turn it off. But you say, "Wait, wait, wait! It's just about to get good!"

Well, here's where our spiritual journey gets good my friends. Just when we're about to throw up our hands and declare there's no hope, God gives us the solution to the ultimate impossible situation. Ephesians 2:4-7 is the Master's solution to all of mankind's problems. "*But God*, being *rich in mercy*, because of the great love with which he loved us, even when we were dead in our trespasses, made us *alive together* with Christ—by grace you have been saved— and raised us up with him and seated us with him in the heavenly places in Christ Jesus, so that in the coming ages he might show the immeasurable *riches of his grace* in kindness toward us in Christ Jesus."(ESV)

Paul starts to turn this tragic ship around with two little words, "But God". At this point, only in my head, it sounds a little like a varsity cheer squad, "Hold on. Wait a minute. Gotta put the Lord in it!" (Forgive me if that image borders on sacrilege, but it's just how my mind works.) Those two little words change everything!

Then we find out God is rich in mercy (verse 4). That is, He doesn't give us the wrath we deserve. Well, why would He do that? Because of the great love with which He loved us. How do we know that love was a great love? Because He loved us even when we were dead in our sins, undeserving of love. And then, as if that great love were not enough, He 1) made us alive with Christ, 2) raised us up with Christ, and 3) seated us with Christ. We are just as alive, just as raised, just as seated as Jesus! Crazy right?

But why? Why would God do all of this for undeserving sinners? Well, Paul tells us in verse 7, "So that in the coming ages he might show the immeasurable riches of his grace in kindness toward us in Christ Jesus." God does it just to show off! And do you know what He shows off? He shows us the immeasurable riches of His grace, the giving of good things that we do not deserve. Rich in mercy and rich in grace, that's my Father!

Goldilocks and Highway 492

When I was growing up we had a
Shetland pony named Goldilocks. And one of
my favorite things to do as a child was to get into
a two-wheeled buggy pulled by Goldi and ride up
the paved road, about a half mile or so, to Uncle
Rudy's house. Uncle Rudy is Dad's brother, and
his two boys, T.Y. and Brandon, were some of
mine and my brother, Cody's, favorite playmates
growing up. We would all take turns driving and
riding in the little buggy around and around
Uncle Rudy's yard.

One Sunday afternoon as T.Y. got out of
the buggy leaving me to hold the reins,
something spooked Goldi. It could have been a
screen door slamming. It could have been a kid
stepping on a limb or a toy in the yard. Heck, it
could have been Goldilocks own meaness that
scared her (more on this later), who knows?

Anyway, she spooked, bounded down the steep hill in Uncle Rudy's front yard, and made a hard right turn onto State Highway 492.

Highway 492 is the busiest road connecting Union and Sebastopol, Mississippi. I mean, there may be eight or ten cars a *day* that drive up and down this road. But do you know how many cars it takes to have a real bad accident with a little crippled boy and a Shetland pony buggy? Not but one. To add to the tension, Goldilocks had two young foals back in the pasture at our house, and she meant not to be deterred in returning to them.

As we turned onto the blacktop and picked up speed, Dad came racing down the driveway to try and intercept us. (That is a wonderful picture of a loving father, who, seeing his helpless child in a desperately impossible situation, springs into action.) But Goldi, as we say, was huntin' some yonder, and Dad couldn't quite get there in time.

As we passed, he said the only thing one could say in a moment like that, "Hold on!" Now, Dad yelling, "Hold on!" in that situation had to have been one of the most over-statements of the obvious in all of human history. "I am!" was all I could manage in response.

Now, Goldilocks had traveled Highway 492 so many times that she not only knew her way home, but she even knew to stay in the right-hand lane. We even met several cars headed in the opposite direction. As I waved feverishly for help, they waved right back...just being friendly, 'cause that's what Southerners do.

I wish at this point in the story that I could say that it was I who sprang into action. And that, just like a scene out of some John Wayne movie, I leapt from the seat of that runaway buggy onto the pony's back. Then, I grabbed both reins, twisted her head to side, bit her ear, wrestled her to the ground, and ended the whole fiasco. But that's not what happened. I have cerebral palsy. I was utterly helpless.

What happened was, Uncle Rudy jumped into his 1970-something Volkswagen van and chased us down. Do ya'll remember Roscoe P. Coltrane on "The Dukes of Hazzard" saying "I'm in hot pursuit!"? Well, Uncle Rudy was! He passed me and Goldilocks on the left-hand side, positioned the van in front of us, then slowed and slowed, until an impatient Goldi tried to re-pass him on the left-hand side. Then, in one fluid motion, Uncle Rudy slammed the van in park, jumped from vehicle and grabbed the reins, saving me from what could have been a tragic ending.

Now the punch-line to the story is that when Dad arrived on the scene moments later, the first thing he said when he got in the buggy was, "Don't tell your Mom." Ya'll also must know that Mom knew everything before we got home because my sister, Sharman, saw the whole thing standing at the end of our driveway. But the moral of the story is much greater.

When it comes to our sin, when it comes to our great debt, when it comes to our right standing before a holy God, we are all much like my situation in that buggy. We are all on a runaway evil Shetland pony buggy ride bound for hell, and utterly helpless to do anything about it. And if we are no longer so destined, it is not because we with determination and strength have grabbed the reins and taken control of our spiritual well-being. It is because we have been rescued. It is because we've been saved.

Ephesians 2:8-9 reads, "For it is *by grace you have been saved*, through faith—and this is not from yourselves, it is the gift of God— *not by works, so that no one can boast.*"

Uncle Oren's Bow

"*T*here are rare individuals in this world who stand head and shoulders above the rest; men who have strong convictions, high ethics, moral integrity, and binding commitment to friendships. These individuals walk alone and talk softly, leading by quiet example.

I met such a man many years ago, a man who changed my views of the world and people, a man who I cherished and was proud to call my friend. That man was Jerry Oren Pierce, a pillar of strength and ideals in the traditional bowhunting community.

We have all seen or heard about his famous Choctaw recurves, with the now famous 'Pierce Points,' his trademark finger jointed riser. Jerry never sold them, rather, he gave them to people who he felt should have one, or donated them to bowhunting organizations around the country for auction items. They brought much needed monies into the coffers of many organizations, and they adorn many a wall for their sheer beauty and uncompromising craftsmanship that only Jerry could improve on."

This is an excerpt from the Editors Note in the August/September 1999 issue of "Traditional Bowhunter Magazine" by T.J. Conrads. This great man of which he speaks was known simply to me as "Uncle Oren". He was the brother of my maternal grandmother Norma Pierce Winstead. He always seemed to me a huge man, and reminded me of Richard Mull's character "Bull" on the sit-com "Night Court". He had a slouch in his walk, a twinkle in his eye, and a great sense of humility.

I remember as a young boy the day Uncle Oren delivered to me at my parents' home my very own youth version of his "Choctaw recurve". I had no idea how priceless what I had is. (For I still have this fine piece of craftsman-ship.) Only three on the youth models were ever made, and I remember my parents repeatedly reminding me to "take care of it".

When I married into Kelly's family and found out that her dad and many of his friends were avid bow hunters, I took my bow to show them. It was like an angelic glow had shone down when they found out I was Jerry Oren Pierce's great-nephew. I vividly remember Danny's friend Matt holding my bow, starring at it, commenting on the detail and the craftsmanship.

Ephesians 2:10 says that, "We are (God's) *workmanship*, created in Christ Jesus for good works, which God prepared beforehand, that we should walk in them."(ESV) I gotta tell ya, having this disability yet knowing that I am God's handiwork, and that He created me with more intricacies than one of Uncle Oren's bows, is of great comfort and peace to me.

From the little boy who was left out of such simple childhood activities as doing the hokey-pokey, to the grown man husband and father that still struggles with issues of inadequacy, how sweet to know...

"I have a Maker
He formed my heart.
Before even time began
My life was in His hands.
He knows my name.
He knows my every thought.
He sees each tear that falls
And hears me when I call."

Practical

Advice

From

James

Diaper Disaster

I'm proud to report that I've changed my share of diapers. I have never been one to use my disability to get out of doing stuff. But, I gotta tell you, with the arrival of our firstborn, there was a great temptation to shirk this responsibility. The Amazing Kelly let it be known in no uncertain terms that I would "find a way", just like so many other things in my life, to handle this duty. (Pun obviously intended.)

Jeff Foxworthy once commented, "Changing a baby's diaper is a lot like opening a present from your grandmother. You don't know what's inside...but you're pretty sure you're not gonna like it." Truer words have never been spoken. To make diaper changing wheelchair friendly, we fashioned a changing table in our bedroom out of a trunk raised off the floor on 4x4s, making it the perfect height to change diapers from a seated position. I may not have changed half the diapers of my children, but I'd be willing to bet I changed at least the average of the average husband and father.

I became proficient, at least by cerebral palsy standards, at changing my son's diapers, managing to get peed on only a couple of times. I was able to arrange my teaching schedule to lecture night classes at the college so that I could keep Will while Kelly worked during the day. Remember in Mark 5, when Jesus healed the man with a legion of demons, that the townspeople came and found the man "sitting there, dressed and in his right mind"? Well, even though it felt sometimes like a legion of demons had attacked our home while Kelly was at work, Will and I were always alive, and usually clothed and in our right mind when she arrived home.

Things changed when Anna Morgan came along. I, as a middle aged man with cerebral palsy, kept two children, both under the age of three and in diapers, at home alone by myself three mornings a week. It was, to say the least, challenging. It only lasted one school year, but before it started I figured I'd have enough material to anchor a book by itself. Problem is, it all happened so fast, I didn't have time to write it all down.

One evening after dinner, Kelly asked me to get the baby ready for bed while she cleaned the kitchen. I went into our bedroom, laid Anna Morgan on the accessible changing table, took her clothes off and prepared to change her diaper. To do so, I took my feet off the footrest of the wheelchair, placed them on the floor, and scooched to the edge of my seat so that I could reach the necessary items as needed. This is a very important detail…that would come back to haunt me later.

As soon as I took Anna Morgan's clothes off, she grabbed both her feet in her hands and said "piggies". She loved for me to play with her toes, and would giggle and coo, much to this father's delight. Instead of the traditional "This little piggy went to market" while counting each toe, however, I said what my Mamaw Winstead taught me: "Little one, lean one, long one, licker-pot, toe-ball, toe-ball, toe-ball!" (By the way, if anyone outside of my immediate family has ever heard of this silliness, please contact me immediately. I would love to research its origins.)

About this time, Will came into the room, noticed the attention his little sister was getting, and immediately wanted his toes "counted". He put his foot up high on the changing table, and balanced on one leg while I played the little game. When he went to put his foot down, he lost his balance and that's when things took a turn for the worse.

Beside the changing table, we had a small wooden TV tray that held a small basket of diapers, wipes, ointment, and baby powder. When Will reached for it to steady himself, he knocked the whole thing ever, causing quite a mess. As he dutifully began cleaning up, and I reached to put things back in their place, my side pressed the joystick controller of my wheelchair setting it into motion. Remember I told ya'll my feet were on the floor? Now, if your feet are on the floor not moving, and the rest your body is in a wheelchair that is…something's gotta give!

I began to fall right towards Will. He was like one of those cartoon characters whose feet are moving, but they're not getting anywhere. He finally kicked it into gear, avoiding being crushed by me, but slamming face-first into the dresser. Kelly heard the commotion and raced to see what was wrong.

Imagine the scene she walked into. I'm lying on the floor in pain. Will's lying on the floor crying. Anna Morgan's crying. There are diapers everywhere, wipes everywhere, bodies everywhere. If a can had exploded, and a thin cloud of baby powder had been hovering in the air, it would've looked like the aftermath of the "Shootout at the OK Corral"!

For the next half hour or so, Anna Morgan was virtually inconsolable. That baby just cried and cried. And remember, she wasn't hurt in the fracas. She remained perfectly safe on the changing table. But she witnessed the whole thing, and she saw her father hurting.

I'll ask a simple question: Do the things that break God's heart also break your heart? Do the things that break the Father's heart break your heart? Do the things that moved Jesus to compassion, move you to act?

I truly believe that one of the things that cause the Father the most heart ache is that we get the giggles over so many things that cause Him grief. I also believe that one of the things that breaks His heart is how we treat other human beings. God has given us so much beauty on this earth; mountain grandeur, majestic waterfalls, picturesque sunsets. But you will never see a single thing on this planet that is more beautiful in the eyes of God than a human being. And the vilest human on the planet is closer to the image of God than any other creature.

This is why we are sternly warned in James 2:1-4, "My brothers and sisters, believers in our glorious Lord Jesus Christ *must not show favoritism.* Suppose a man comes into your meeting wearing a gold ring and fine clothes, and a poor man in filthy old clothes also comes in. If you show special attention to the man wearing fine clothes and say, 'Here's a good seat for you,' but say to the poor man, 'You stand there' or 'Sit on the floor by my feet,' *have you not discriminated among yourselves and become judges with evil thoughts?"*

You of All People

I remember sitting in Mrs. Theresa Blount's seventh grade homeroom class talking to my good buddy Jeremy Blackwell about, well, whatever seventh grade boys talk about, when Tamella Mazingo walked in. Tamella was naturally tall, and had hit her growth spurt before the rest of us. Jeremy, for the whole classroom to hear, said, "Here comes that amazon!"

I'll pause here to plead a little ignorance. Jeremy had probably seen "Amazon Women From Mars" or some such B-movie nonsense on cable or satellite TV, and thought the reference would be funny. Quite honestly, I don't even think I knew what the word "amazon" meant. I mean, I'd never seen the movie. Cable literally didn't (doesn't) run out to Conehatta, and Mom and Dad didn't get satellite until 2009.

After Jeremy said, "Here comes that amazon," he laughed. And even though I didn't really know what he meant, since he laughed, I laughed. Then, as kids often do, I repeated him. "Yeah, look at that amazon," I said. Then I laughed, and Jeremy laughed, and we all had a good laugh.

Tamella, however, was not amused. She went storming from the room in search of some authority figure. Luckily for Jeremy and I, the principal was not at school that day, and the only authority figure Tamela could find was the band director, Mr. Germany. After a few minutes, Mr.Germany stuck his head in the room and said, "You boys go to the office and wait for me there."

So we did. But I gotta tell ya, we weren't real nervous about it. I mean, first of all, we had just called someone a name. It wasn't like we had beaten someone up and taken their lunch money or anything. And secondly, it was the band director! Who's afraid of the band director? Jeremy and I were so calm and cool, so not nervous, that I remember us literally playing a hand or two of cards in the office while we waited for Mr.Germany to arrive.

That is when things took a turn! When Mr. Germany sat down in the office in front of us, he started in on Jeremy. I mean he chewed him up one side and down the other. It may have been one of the most severe tongue lashings I've ever witnessed. I just remember thinking the whole time, "Oh, no. It's gonna be my turn next."

And it was. But my turn turned out to be very different. After Mr. Germany had finished with Jeremy, he caught his breath and turned and looked at me. The look in his eyes had turned from anger to disappointment. He just shook his head and said, "And you, Justin. You of all people…"

That's all it took. That's all I needed to understand his full meaning. It crushed my little spirit…but I got the point. "You of all people…You, who knows what it's like to be different. You, who knows what it's like to made fun of by other kids because of those differences. You of all people ought to know better."

James is essentially saying the same thing in chapter two. "Listen, my dear brothers and sisters: *Has not God chosen those who are poor in the eyes of the world to be rich in faith* and to inherit the kingdom he promised those who love him? *But you have dishonored the poor. Is it not the rich who are exploiting you? Are they not the ones who are dragging you into court?* Are they not the ones who are blaspheming the noble name of him to whom you belong?"

You can almost hear the disappointment in his voice, can't you? "You of all people…who are poor in the eyes of the world. You of all people…who know what it's like to be exploited. You of all people…who know what it's like to be drug into court. You of all people ought to know better!"

Notice how the Apostle Paul concludes his second letter to Timothy:

"Do your best to come to me quickly, for *Demas*, because he loved this world, has deserted me and has gone to Thessalonica. *Crescens* has gone to Galatia, and *Titus* to Dalmatia. Only *Luke* is with me. Get *Mark* and bring him with you, because he is helpful to me in my ministry. I sent *Tychicus* to Ephesus. When you come, bring the cloak that I left with *Carpus* at Troas, and my scrolls, especially the parchments.

Alexander the metalworker did me a great deal of harm. The Lord will repay him for what he has done. You too should be on your guard against him, because he strongly opposed our message…

Greet *Priscilla* and *Aquila* and the household of *Onesiphorus*. *Erastus* stayed in Corinth, and I left *Trophimus* sick in Miletus. Do your best to get here before winter. *Eubulus* greets you, and so do *Pudens, Linus, Claudia* and all the brothers and sisters. The Lord be with your spirit. Grace be with you all."

Did you see it? In these verses Paul mentions seventeen different people who have impacted his life. Here is Paul in a cold dungeon, chained like a common criminal, knowing he is nearing the end of his life, and what he thinks about is relationships. And my point is: you'll never meet anyone who isn't important to God.

Let us never for a moment believe we are doing God a favor by entering His kingdom. Let us never think that we ever got our act together enough for God to save us. It is by grace alone, through faith alone, in Christ alone that salvation is possible. And because of that, let us never act like anything more than beggars simply telling other beggars where to find bread. We of all people…

The Letter of the Law

*O*ne night after supper at the Fisher house in early August 2013 the following conversation ensued:

Will: Dad, let's go for a walk.

Me: OK. One last walk, just the boys, before you start kindergarten tomorrow. (Great Godly, father/son bonding time is gonna happen on this walk, I can feel it!.......half an hour later, we're on our way back.)

Me: Let's make this our back to school tradition.

Will: What's a tradition?

Me: You know like *every* year on Christmas Eve we go to big church, and then to Waffle House for supper. That's a tradition, cause we do it every year.

Will: Dad, can we make Super Hero costumes part of our tradition?

So maybe Will understood the definition of tradition, but not the *spirit* of tradition that I was attempting to foster. James 2:8-11 reads, "If you really keep the royal law found in Scripture, 'Love your neighbor as yourself,' you are doing right. But if you show favoritism, you sin and are convicted by the law as lawbreakers. For whoever keeps the whole law and yet stumbles at just one point is guilty of breaking all of it. For he who said, 'You shall not commit adultery,' also said, 'You shall not murder.' If you do not commit adultery but do commit murder, you have become a lawbreaker."

I think maybe here James is referring to the Spirit of the law rather than the letter of the law. And we would all do well to follow the guidance of the Holy Spirit when it comes to our relationships with others.

Matt's Mouse

*T*he Amazing Kelly may deserve the "Wife of the Year" award for Christmas 2011 when she bought me a crossbow. I had been talking about buying one for some time, but never had pulled the trigger, pardon the pun. Having a disability, it just seemed a good way for me to extend deer season beyond gun hunting. Kelly knew that there was an opportunity for me to hunt coming up at a "bow only" area, and she actually surprised me before Christmas Day with this great gift.

My first opportunity to try my skills with my new toy, was with my friend Matt at a hunting club he belongs to in south Georgia called "The Paradise". I'll pause here to make very clear that the name does not refer to the human accommodations. It's called "The Paradise" because it is hog heaven. It is swampy, nasty, muddy, over-grown...wait, was I describing where the hogs sleep or where the people sleep?

The camp, maybe I should put that in quotations, is really a couple of storage buildings on the slab of an old house-place, surrounded by abandoned trailers demolished by weather and left by previous hunters at the club. One of the storage buildings is larger and set up a bit like a bunk house. The other is considerably smaller and is Matt's "private residence". There is electricity in the storage buildings, but no running water inside. In fact, going to the bathroom in the middle of the night involves shoes and a flashlight!

I'll take a minute here to tell you that my hunting buddy Matt is a manly man. He's more or less a confirmed bachelor. His best friend is what most of us consider to be the ugliest dog on the planet, a German Wirehaired Pointer named

"Montana". He has a real job, but he could easily live off the land if need be. Matt grows his own vegetables, and hunts and fishes for meat. By the way, when he's hunting, virtually everything that moves, he does so with bow and arrow he made himself. And when it comes to "The Paradise", he loves the place.

After the first day of the hunt, we ate a big supper and sat around the campfire and chatted until it was time for bed. (Morning comes early when you're at "The Paradise".) Matt helped me settle in at the bunk house, said goodnight, and then headed to his "cabin" about fifty yards away. I sat down on the bunk and was about to pull my boots off when, you guessed it, a mouse ran out from under my bed, along the base of the wall and underneath the bunk on the other side of the room.

Now, to be clear, this was not like a sewer rat the size of a small dog or anything. It was just a field mouse. And, while the amenities at "The Paradise" are a long way from "The Four Seasons", or a Motel 6 for that matter, the place didn't appear to be over-run with the furry critters. So I decided the best course of action was just to steel my nerves and deal with it, for two main reasons.

First of all, it was just a mouse, right? And what is a mouse but a squirrel with no fluffy tail and a PR problem. Squirrels don't bother me. I was literally surrounded by dozens of them while I was hunting. Secondly, I decided that if I was gonna go hunting with manly man Matt, a mouse in the bunk house was just, well, part of it.

So I decided I would be a manly man too. I mean, when I told people I was going wild hog hunting down in south Georgia with my crossbow, I felt manly. When I sat around the campfire and drank black coffee and told of the adventures of past hunts, I felt manly. When I sat out in the rain in my camouflage and waited for a wild animal to come within spitting distance to harvest and provide meat for my family, I felt manly. But, ya'll, when that mouse came back out in full view and ran underneath the bed I was sitting on...I was done being manly!

I got on my crutches, walked outside and, according to Matt, screamed like a little girl. In my defense, Matt was in his cabin fifty yards away sleeping with earplugs and a snoring dog. I was just trying to get his attention. After a few minutes, I saw a light come on, and a few minutes later, he was walking up the steps to the bunkhouse. "You rang?," he said, grinning sheepishly. I said, "Hey, brother. You can make fun of me all you want to, but I'm not gonna be able to sleep with your little friend in there."

And he did. He made fun of me quite a bit. He called me some names that I'll not repeat in a Christian devotional book. Some were clever, some were funny, some were well...true. He gave me a good ribbing, all in good fun.

And then do you know what he did? He traded places with me! He packed up all my stuff, my sleeping bag and everything and moved me to his private cabin. And, knowing Montana would be up all night with a stranger in the room, Matt moved to the bunkhouse. Now Matt's place was no Ritz Carlton, but there were no signs of mice, and I spent the next two nights in relative peace, quiet and comfort.

I know it's not a perfect allegory, but it does give us just a little glimpse into what Jesus did for us. What was that? Well, He traded places with us. That should have been us on that cross. All of the pain, suffering, torture and humiliation should have been poured out on us for our sins. 1 John 2:2 tells us, "(Jesus) is the atoning sacrifice for our sins, and not only for ours but also for the sins of the whole world."

Did Matt make fun of me because I'm not as manly as he is? You bet. Will God make fun of us because we are not righteous and holy as He is? No, but it is on that premise that we will be judged. But never fear. If you have accepted the precious gift of Christ's atoning sacrifice, then God will declare the debt of your sin paid in full. How should we respond to a love like that? James 2:12-13 tells us, "Speak and act as those who are going to be judged by the law that gives freedom, because judgment without mercy will be shown to anyone who has not been merciful. *Mercy triumphs over judgment*!"

And after we pass from death unto life, God gives us a mansion with Him in Heaven...with no mice.

Glimpses of

His Grace

Snatched Back

*O*n February 6th, 2013, I added my 1000th Facebook friend. Her name is Kelli Evans Brown. She is married to Donnell Brown of Throckmorton, Texas, and together they run a large cattle ranch. I met Kelli when I was in the ninth grade at Union High School and she was a freshman at the Oklahoma State University.

Our one on one conversations over the next four years might have reached a total sum of one hour in duration, but this lady, like so many other people over the years, unknowingly had a profound impact on my life. None of them set out with a goal of injecting confidence into the life of a young man with cerebral palsy. No, they did it just by being themselves.

Like I said, this all starts at Union High School, Union, Mississippi, 1987. At the time, UHS offered very few elective courses. In fact, the way I remember it, the girls went to "Home Ec" class and the guys went to "Vo Ag" class. "Vo Ag" stands for Vocational Agriculture, and while none of us ever intended to become farmers, er, um, vocational agriculturalist, we were certainly not going to spend our time learning to cook and sew. The Vo Ag teacher was Mr. Mark Savell. Whether Mr. Savell took a special interest in me because I was in a wheelchair, or because I was simultaneously his third and fourth cousin (he'd have to explain it to you), really doesn't matter. The fact is that he did, and it changed my life forever.

Mr. Savell encouraged me to get involved in the FFA, Future Farmers of America. Again, I saw no farming in my future, but the FFA opened up a world for me I had never known previously: competition. While many of my able bodied friends were involved in athletic competition, in the FFA I found an outlet for my competitive spirit. The first competition I took part in was called "Creed Speaking". Mr. Savell required all of us as freshman to recite the FFA Creed for a grade in his Vo Ag class. I figured if I had to learn it anyway, I may as well learn it well, and get to get out of school one afternoon to perform at the District Competition. After more than twenty-five years, I still remember the first two paragraphs of the Creed:

> "I believe in the future of farming, with a faith born not of words but of deeds - achievements won by present and past generations of farmers; in the promise of better days through better ways, even as the better things we now enjoy have come to us from the struggles of former years.
> I believe that to live and work on a good farm is pleasant as well as challenging; for I know the joys and discomforts of farm life, and hold an inborn fondness for those associations which, even in hours of discouragement, I cannot deny."

Yep. Just typed that whole thing from memory. Then I Googled to see if I got it right. Only missed one little prepositional phrase. (Probably the same one I missed twenty-five years ago which caused me to place second in the competition and miss a trip to the state finals.) But I, as they say, had been "bug-bit" and I got so involved in the FFA my freshman year that I was nominated to receive the "Star Greenhand Award". The award was given at the end-of-the-year FFA banquet. We were also told that the national student president of the organization would be speaking at the UHS FFA banquet. That person was Kelli Evans.

I won the "Star Greenhand Award" that night, but that's not what made my night special. After the banquet was over, Kelli came over to congratulate me. And ya'll as Kelli Evans, THE national president of the FFA, with that long blonde hair and big eyes and that blue and gold corduroy jacket on approached, it felt like she was moving in slow motion! I, a freshman at a little poe-dunk high school, was carrying on a conversation with a beautiful, intelligent, successful college girl! And she initiated it! She said that she'd heard great things about me, and I learned that she was majoring in Agricultural Economics.

Well, fast-forward four years or so. I did everything there was to do in FFA. I was Chapter Officer, livestock judge, parliamentary procedure contestant, District Officer candidate, state extemporaneous public speaking contestant, and eventually State Officer. Because of my involvement, I applied for and received one of the prestigious college scholarships offered by the FFA. The only requirement was that I major in some area of agriculture.

What do you think I chose? That's right...Agricultural Economics! Now it didn't hurt that I enjoyed my one semester of high school economics (thanks Coach Johnson), but that certainly wasn't the main reason. I thought to myself, "If ALL of the girls majoring in Agricultural Economics are like Kelli Evans...that's EXACTLY where I need to be!" And that, dear friends, is how I chose my major.

There are two glaring ironies here. The first is that when I arrived at Mississippi State to start my junior year after transferring from East Central Community College, I realized there were VERY few girls majoring in Ag. Econ. (And I can assure you NONE of them were like Kelli Evans.) The second irony is that these days part of my job is advising students and occasionally one of them will ask me to help them choose a major. My response, "Well, let me tell you how NOT to do it."

Awhile back someone told me, "If you like where you are, you can't complain about how you got there." Can I just tell you...I LOVE where I am! I have an amazing wife, kids, job, friends, church family, the list goes on and on.

So Romans 8:28 is still true. Even when we follow our own selfish priorities, even when we don't make wise decisions, even when we stray, God really is working all things together for our good and His glory. And He can snatch our lives back on the path that most glorifies Him despite our choices. My friend David Balzer, pastor of Grace Presbyterian Church near Stone Mountain, Georgia, once prayed for me, "Father, help Justin to have true humility. Help him to know that You can be glorified through imperfect works with imperfect motives."

And if I hadn't majored in Ag. Econ. there are people I would have never met and things I might never have experienced. So thanks David Mancil who introduced me to hunting. I now spend many happy hours enjoying God's creation. And thanks Dr. Little who taught me how to be a Christian witness in the classroom. And thanks Dr. Reinschmiedt who taught me how to treat students like people. And thanks to Dr. Herndon who taught me that as a man, sometimes things don't go your way, and you suck it up and deal with it!

And thanks be to God, the giver of "Every good and perfect gift…from the Father of the heavenly lights, who does not change like shifting shadows." (James 1:17)

Snatched Away

I'll begin with a similar disclaimer as that of my first book; this story is *not* about me! I have in fact hesitated to include it in this collection for fear that it might be misinterpreted. This story is about the sovereignty of God who owns "the cattle on a thousand hills" (Ps. 50:10), and who uses the gifts and resources stewarded by His people to glorify Himself.

I cannot tell you where this story begins. The Lord our God is the Alpha and Omega, the beginning and the end, so history really is His-story. I can only tell you where this story begins from my perspective. I do, however, know that I am only one small cog in this giant wheel of God redeeming His people unto Himself.

For me it began when a couple of colleagues at Jefferson State Community College asked if I would be a guest speaker at a youth leadership conference they were helping to organize. I'll stop right here to tell you that this kind of thing is not exactly my cup of tea. Don't get me wrong, I'm perfectly comfortable speaking in front of large groups and I teach students every day, so the size or demographic of the crowd didn't bother me. It was the particular topic that I was unsure of.

I have, for the most part, gotten away from the motivational or inspirational speaking genre to focus on Biblical teaching. However, a few months before I was approached by my colleagues, I was invited to speak at a church on Father's Day. I shared the story of Nehemiah and talked about "Rebuilding the Wall". I decided that I could tell the story from a historical perspective to the students, and use it to teach sound leadership principles like facing adversity, teamwork and motivation.

Little did I know that God was already at

work in this endeavor. At a planning meeting a few weeks before the conference, I announced my topic "Rebuilding the Wall". I wish I had a picture of my colleagues' faces! Their jaws literally dropped. Unbeknownst to me they had already named (and had T-shirts made for) the conference entitled "Scaling the Wall". I knew then that God was at work. I just didn't know, and may never know this side of Heaven, to what extent.

I was scheduled to speak at a Friday mid-morning session, which was *perfect*. I could drop Anna Morgan off at Mother's Day Out, drive to the conference a half hour away, do my thing and be back in plenty of time to pick her up. However, just a few days before the conference I was asked to swap with another speaker and do the afternoon session. Aaaarrrgggghhh!

Nobody wants to be a speaker on Friday afternoon. Everybody's got the weekend on their minds. Plus I'd have to make other arrangements for Anna Morgan to be picked up. It was, or so I thought, bad news all around. But as a favor to my colleagues, I agreed. I would eventually realize that everything I'd ever taught about Romans 8:28 was still true.

When I arrived at the conference, I learned that I would be the key note speaker at the closing assembly. This is it! The big finish everyone had been waiting for. It was also a larger crowd than any other session because parents and sponsors were there. Now, generally speaking, high school students don't spend their money on books...but their parents and sponsors do! I was warmly received, the talk went well, the crowd laughed in all the right places, and I even sold a few books afterward. All in all it turned out to be a pretty good afternoon.

On the way home I stopped by the bank to deposit the checks I received from book sales, but I kept the cash knowing that I'd need some for the weekend. That night I took the family out to eat cheap Mexican food (a Fisher family favorite), and used some of that cash to pay the bill. I even set aside some cash that I was going to contribute as part of a love offering for a couple in our church Life Connection class who were moving away.

The next night, at the going away party there was food, fun and fellowship. As the party was winding down, I overheard a lady in our class talking about the upcoming mission trip in which her and her family were going to participate. She was asked about all the particular costs of travel and food and lodging, etc. She said that the family had steadily been raising support, but time was getting close to leave and they were still short. Then another member of the class asked, "So how much more do you need?"

Now, I'm gonna go ahead and tell ya'll...I was already planning to contribute to the mission trip, but it would not have been a significant contribution. And while I certainly understand that "every little bit helps" and "many hands make light work", I was not prepared for what was about to happen. In the brief instant it took my friend to answer that question, I must've said a thousand prayers. They all sounded something like, "Lord, please let it be a huge number!" "Please let it be like $5,000 or something so that I can't possibly be expected to give it all."

But wouldn't you know it; this family's mission trip fund was short *exactly* the amount of cash that I had in my wallet! Ain't that just like Jesus? I told my friend this story and gave them the money. They cried, we hugged, and we were simply overcome by God's grace, and provision, and timing, and love.

2 Corinthians 9:7 reads, "Each of you should give what you have decided in your heart to give, not reluctantly or under compulsion, for God loves a cheerful giver." I must admit, if someone had told me that God would require *all* the cash I'd received from book sales that day, I would probably not have been very cheerful. Even though I'd seen God's hand at work from the planning of the talk, to the increase in crowd size that led to an increase in book sales, I was still a bit reluctant to hand over all of my cash even to this missionary endeavor.

The point I've learned, and the one I must share is this; it's *all* His anyway. From the job (where I met the colleagues who invited me to speak), to the gift of gab I've been given, to the ability to write and publish and sell books, to the van I drove to and from the conference, to my family I took out to eat cheap Mexican food…*it's all His*. It *all* belongs to God! We are simply stewards for a short time. And He can snatch it away anytime He sovereignly chooses.

God help us to be generous with what we've been given so that in due time we might hear the words of our Savior recorded in Matthew 25:21, "Well done, good and faithful servant! You have been faithful with a few things; I will put you in charge of many things. Come and share your master's happiness!"

Snatched Out

*F*or those of you keeping score at home, I ain't the only one that was raised at Route 1, Conehatta, Mississippi. I've got a brother and a sister, and my brother's got a brother and a sister, and then my sister's got two brothers. And for those of you that are too quick with the math, there's only three of us. My little brother, Cody, is six years younger than me, and my sister, Sharman, is just a couple years older. It is she that will be the heroine of this storylet.

January 24, 2013 started out as a typical day at her home. Sharman "keeps children". For those of ya'll who ain't from around here, if we were younger it'd be called "babysitting", and if her clients were richer she'd be a "nanny". At any rate, folks pay her to watch their young-uns while they go off to work. It's a noble profession, and I for one am thankful for those who've watched mine over the years.

Sharman was keeping five babies that day ranging in age from one to four years. They had eaten lunch for the day and were all down for their nap. My sister lit a scented candle in the hall bathroom and prepared to enjoy her lunch and a bit of peace and quiet. She was careful not to place the candle too close to the two tier wrought iron piece of décor where the body sponges and bath cloths were displayed. She was also careful to make sure that it was not within reach of the older children that would surely be in there to use the potty at some point that afternoon.

Or so she thought. After a quick check of the sleeping beauties on the opposite end of the house, Sharman headed towards the kitchen. But before she could arrive, the fire alarm began to blare! She ran to the bathroom to find the bath cloths, body sponges and everything on the stand in flames. She remembers saying out loud, "God help me! God help me!" Sharman first tried to smother the flames with towels. When that didn't work she hurled the flaming stand into the bathtub and ran to the kitchen for the fire extinguisher. She got to the bathroom door and pulled the pin out, or thought she pulled the pin out, and nothing happened! Then it was time to call 911 and get out!

Not just herself, but those five precious babies whose mothers and fathers trust her with their children every day. Here's a quote from Sharman's journaling. "I grabbed my cell phone, dialed 911 and immediately started gathering children. First, I *snatched* up the oldest who was four. I marched her out the door and told her to wait there…Next, I got the youngest, a year old, and put him on my hip. Then, one by one, I basically *snatched* the other three up, like a momma dog, by the nap of their necks and escorted them to the door."

The house received severe smoke damage and had to be gutted down to the studs. Sharman received some severe burns on her left hand that God miraculously healed leaving nary a scar. But the important thing is that my sister and those children are alive and well, and God receives all the glory.

God commands us through the words of Jude 1:23, "Save others by *snatching them from the fire*; to others show mercy, mixed with fear— hating even the clothing stained by corrupted flesh." Are you about your Father's business? Do you believe that hell is real? Are you snatching others from the fire like a momma dog with her puppies? Are you doing so with mercy mixed with fear? Do you hate sin? Does it make you nauseous like the smell of smoke on clothing that lingers after a house fire?

We do so with the utmost humility. "To him who is able to keep you from stumbling and to present you before his glorious presence without fault and with great joy— to the only God our Savior be glory, majesty, power and authority, through Jesus Christ our Lord, before all ages, now and forevermore! Amen." (Jude 1:24-25)

Snatched Up

I enjoy listening to good preaching. I listen to a lot of good preaching on Moody Radio. The habit started several years ago when I taught evening classes in the summertime. About the time I would start home, John MacArthur and the "Grace to You" program would begin. MacArthur quickly became, and still is, one of my favorite Bible teachers. I then discovered other good preachers on Moody Radio. Folks like Ravi Zacharias, and Alistair Begg, always seemed to be able to use God's Word to stir my heart and mind. I still listen to Christian music, secular music and talk radio with political and social commentary, but more and more, my radio dial is tuned to Moody.

One day Will and I were loading into the van, and as soon as I cranked up, James MacDonald's voice could be heard on the radio and he said, "Jesus is coming back soon!" The following conversation ensued:

Will: Jesus is coming back soon?

Me: Yep. One day God will say "ENOUGH! Enough death. Enough pain. Enough hurt. Enough tears. Enough!" And He'll say "Son, go get your children." And then Jesus will snatch us up into heaven with Him and we'll have the biggest party EVER! Won't that be cool?

Will: Nope...

And I quickly realized that going to Heaven that summer was not on Will Fisher's agenda. Now, before you giggle too much at young master William, the Bible says in 1 Corinthians 10:12, "If you think you are standing firm, be careful that you don't fall!" The simple truth is that most Christians are as excited about Heaven as a ten year old boy who has just been invited to an all-girl birthday party. Deep down our hearts say, "I guess I'll go...but, if it's all the same, I just as soon stay here."

I posted mine and Will's conversation on Facebook, and a friend of mine pointed out that it might have been my use of the phrase "snatch us up" that had caused Will's reluctance. She mentioned that she didn't like the idea of being "snatched" to anywhere, much less up into the air. I can certainly understand that.

However, I did a little research and the idea of being snatched up is completely accurate. The original Greek lexicon, used in the New Testament some thirteen times is "harpazo", and it means "to snatch out or away". It is the word Paul uses in 1 Thessalonians 4:17 when he writes, "After that, we who are still alive and are left will be *caught up* together with them in the clouds to meet the Lord in the air. And so we will be with the Lord forever."

Another definition of "harpazo" is "to

claim for one's self eagerly". Now that's a definition that Will, and you and I for that matter, should be able to get our minds around. Think about it. If a child finds a sibling playing with their prized toy, their first impulse is to say "Mine!" and *snatch* it away.

I believe this is exactly what Jesus will do. In the fullness of time, when all that is to be fulfilled has been fulfilled, Jesus will say to Satan, "These children are *mine*...and you will persecute them no more!" And then, "In a flash, in the twinkling of an eye, at the last trumpet. For the trumpet will sound, the dead will be raised imperishable, and we will be changed."(1 Cor. 15:52)

After all, for those who are Christians, "Do you not know that your bodies are temples of the Holy Spirit, who is in you, whom you have received from God? *You are not your own; you were bought at a price.*"(1 Cor. 6:19-20a) If we were "bought at a price", then we are indeed His. And if we are His, then He indeed has every right to say "Mine!" and snatch us up to be with Him forever. And about that we should be excited: not as a ten year old boy invited to an all-girl birthday soiree, but a five year old boy on Christmas Eve!

Meditations

on the

Beattitudes

There's Something Hap-pening Here...

I feel that it's been well documented, but I'll go on record once again and say, "I love my wife!" I love the Amazing Kelly for a lot of different reasons. She is beautiful in the face, in the mind, and in the body. She is a great mother to our children. She is an incredible cook. And, above all, she puts up with me, which in and of itself should qualify her for sainthood!

One thing I really appreciate about Kelly in the wife and motherhood realm is that she packs lunches for us. Kelly and I both work in academia, and it makes neither logistical or economic sense for us to eat out at lunch time. Will eats in the cafeteria at the elementary school now, but up until very recently Kelly would fix lunches for two adults and two children every weekday. And the children's lunchtime plastic-ware containers had to be labeled with their names so as not to be lost in the hustle and bustle of pre-K craziness.

Because of the organized chaos that surrounds a life with two small children, I will occasionally open my lunchbox to find a container with someone else's name on it. That is not to say that I have ever taken one of the children's lunches to work. It is simply to point out that in the whirlwind of the morning rush, Kelly will occasionally grab a plastic-ware container that, though clean, still has a child's name stenciled on it in marker.

This occurrence doesn't bother me. Quite the contrary. I kind of enjoy seeing Will's name and thinking of my Buddy Roe, or smiling at the thought of my Lady Bug when I unexpectedly see Anna Morgan's name in my lunchbox. You can imagine my surprise, however, when I opened my lunchbox awhile back and there printed in plain letters on the top of my plastic-ware container were the words, "Turkey Fat".

I'll end the suspense quickly and tell you that contained inside was not turkey fat. It was standard lunchtime fare. But I realized very quickly that one of about three things was going on. Number one, one of my children had a new nickname I didn't know about. ("Yep. There's our oldest. We're real proud of him. He's our Turkey Fat!") Number two, maybe I had a new nickname that I didn't know about. ("Just calling to see when you're coming home. Ok, I love you, Turkey Fat.") Or number three, and this turned out to be the case, there was something going on at my house with turkey fat that I knew nothing about.

Such is the case oftentimes with familiar passages of Scripture. We have read them to the point of ad nausea. We may even have them memorized. But with the proper context and clarity, we might be surprised to find the words have a totally different meaning than we originally thought.

"Blessed are the poor in spirit,
for theirs is the kingdom of heaven.
Blessed are those who mourn,
for they will be comforted.
Blessed are the meek,
for they will inherit the earth.
Blessed are those who hunger and thirst
for righteousness,
for they will be filled.
Blessed are the merciful,
for they will be shown mercy.
Blessed are the pure in heart,
for they will see God.
Blessed are the peacemakers,
for they will be called children of God.
Blessed are those who are persecuted
because of righteousness,
for theirs is the kingdom of heaven."

Blessed Are the Poor
Matthew 5:3

*W*ell...if that's the case, then those of us from Mississippi must be blessed beyond measure! My home state is indeed pretty low on the totem pole. U.S. Census Bureau data shows that the state of Mississippi has the lowest average household income and the highest rate of poverty in the entire country. Well, at least we're #1 in one thing right? Oh, no. Mississippi also ranks tops in teenage pregnancy and illiteracy.

I'll pause here to say that I indeed get teased a lot while living in Alabama about being from Mississippi. People say things like, "Oh, you're from Mississippi? How do you like this electricity we've got here?" But I'm quick to remind folks that when I moved from Mississippi to Alabama I raised the average intelligence level of both states. Some of them get it. Mostly, folks from Alabama say, "Thank goodness for Mississippi...at least we're not 50th!"

Being poor in Mississippi is indeed something to reckon with. I've heard people say things like, "We were so poor growing up…:

- We didn't even have enough money to *pay attention*."

- We had a house so small, you had to go outside to change your *mind*."

- We used to go down to Kentucky Fried Chicken and lick *other* people's fingers."

However, to interpret Matthew 5:3 as "God will bless those who are financially impoverished" would be poor theology. (No pun intended.) In fact, the verse itself clarifies. It doesn't say, "Blessed are the poor in finances." It says, "Blessed are the poor in *spirit*." Blessed are the spiritually poor. Blessed are those who have declared spiritual bankruptcy. Blessed are those who have come to the end of themselves and, in doing so, cried out to God for their spiritual "savings plan".

Why? Because clinging to Jesus as Savior and Lord means realizing that we have nothing of any spiritual value dwelling inherently inside us. We must come to the point where we say, "Not that we are sufficient of ourselves to think anything as of ourselves; but our sufficiency is of God"(2 Cor. 3:5, KJV).

I sometimes know not whether to laugh or cry when someone declares the Christian worldview to be height of arrogance. "How could you claim that your way is the only way, and that you've got it all figured out?" they ask. No, the true follower of Christ has relinquished all authority and control and declared, "I have nothing to bring to the table."

Christianity is the only group, club, or organization that I know of where the only requirement for membership is to admit that you aren't qualified to join. Blessed are the poor in spirit, for theirs is the kingdom of Heaven.

Blessed Are Those Who Cry
Matthew 5:4

"*B*lessed are those who don't have any money and cry about it. Got it!" Makes sense doesn't it. Heck, if you didn't have any money you'd cry, too! But, again, we're back to "Turkey Fat". There is a much deeper meaning, and much deeper implications than just simple weeping. We're not talking about an "I'm sorry I got caught" kind of sorrow. And we're also not talking about crying for show.

In this, Jesus' Sermon on the Mount, the Beattitudes follow and build upon one another. Jesus in essence says, "Blessed are the spiritually poor, who realize their inadequacy before a holy God, and who mourn over their lost condition." It's the only thing that makes sense. Once we realize that we're woefully inept to earn our way in to God's favor, and once we realize that our natural tendencies have offended the Almighty

Creator of the universe, mourning is the only logical response.

In fact the Bible says it's not only logical, it's positive. The Apostle Paul declares in 2 Corinthians 7:9-11, "...Now I am happy, not because you were made sorry, but because *your sorrow led you to repentance*. For you became *sorrowful* as God intended and so were not harmed in any way by us. *Godly sorrow brings repentance that leads to salvation and leaves no regret,* but worldly sorrow brings death. See what this *godly sorrow* has produced in you: what earnestness, what eagerness to clear yourselves, what indignation, what alarm, what longing, what concern, what readiness to see justice done. At every point you have proved yourselves to be innocent in this matter."

Blessed are the Weak
Matthew 5:5

A few chapters ago I told ya'll about
Goldilocks running away with me down
Highway 492. Anyone who does not believe that
God has a sense of humor has never had any
dealings with the combination Shetland ponies
and children. I really believe that Shetland
ponies are one of God's great jokes on humanity.
I think that we as humans, in our finite wisdom,
have looked at children (little people) and looked
at Shetland ponies (little horses) and in our
ignorance paired the two.

Shetland ponies are evil. I've never met
one that wouldn't rather bite you than look at
you, or that wouldn't rather kick you than let you
ride. And for those ponies that did allow a child
to sit in the saddle, rest assured they were
looking for a clothesline or a low hanging tree
branch to drag them off on. Shetland ponies

should come with a warning label: KEEP OUT OF REACH OF CHILDREN. But it's worse than that. I really think that if God had not chosen to represent evil in the Garden Eden in the form of a serpent…His second choice was a Shetland.

Even the name "Goldilocks" carries some irony. A pretty princess she was not. Quite the contrary, in fact, she was just mean as a snake. But somewhere in all of his trading, Papaw Fisher had come up with that two-wheeled buggy for Goldi to pull. (The buggy was actually Aunt Bonnie's that was once used with her old horse, Moby Dick.) And, believe it or not, it worked pretty well. That was probably because the children, when seated in the buggy, were far enough away from her head that it prevented her from biting, and the metal frame of the buggy was between you and her hind legs, and that prevented her from kicking.

Oh, it wasn't a perfect system. Maybe one day I'll tell ya'll about the time my baby brother, Cody, got out of the buggy to open a gate, and Goldi grabbed him with her teeth in his chest muscle, and picked him up as high as she could over her head before dropping him to the ground.

Then there was the time, with my sister, Sharman, driving, that we came around the big live-oak tree in the front yard much too fast, and the entire buggy, pony-and-all, flipped upside down. Imagine a turtle on its back, unable to right itself…but weighing six hundred pounds with flashing teeth and hooves.

I'd like to contrast the attitude of that heathen horse with the character of one of my favorite mount's ever, Mr. Wilson. I met Wilson many years ago at Special Equestrians, a therapeutic horseback riding facility near Birmingham. Wilson was the biggest "teddy bear" of a horse anyone could wish for. He weighed, literally, half a ton, was as strong as an ox, but he was just a gentle giant. This horse would follow my wheelchair around like a puppy dog.

Wilson would remain perfectly still while I groomed him, allowing me to lean my body weight on him for support while I brushed his back and mane. He would stand patiently in an uncomfortable position next to a fence while I went about the slow process of saddling him. Mr. Wilson would even lean closer to me as I threw my leg over his back from my position on the mounting ramp, so that I wouldn't have to stretch as far. Witnessing this, one day the director of the program said, "You know, that horse wouldn't do that for just anybody."

We could all stand to be a little more like Wilson. You see, one of the neatest things about Wilson is that he *allowed* his strength to be used. He submitted to my control so that I could do what needed to be done. If that animal didn't want to leave his stall, I couldn't have made him. If he had wanted to jerk away and run while I was leading him, he could have. And most of the horses on the face of the earth wouldn't let someone in a wheelchair roll around them and push and pull on them like I did with Wilson.

But Wilson and I had a special relationship. It was a relationship built on trust, not unlike the relationship we as Christians have with our Heavenly Father. I led and Wilson followed. I pulled with the right rein, and he turned right. I squeezed with my legs and he moved faster.

This is the picture of a servant's strength. This is a picture of meekness, which is too often erroneously defined as weakness. It's the essence of allowing oneself to be positioned in order to receive instruction. This is what it means to be a child of God. In John 14:21, Jesus says, "He who has My commandments and *keeps* them, it is he who loves me. And he who loves Me, will be loved by My Father, and I will love him and manifest Myself to him."

Paul said in Galatians 2:20, "I have been *crucified with Christ and I no longer live*, but Christ lives in me. The life I live in the body, I live by faith in the Son of God, who loved me and gave himself for me."

Have you had your daily funeral today?

Blessed Are the Hungry and Thirsty
Matthew 5:6

I can't read these words in Matthew 5:6 without also thinking of Psalm 42:1, "As the deer pants for streams of water, so my soul pants for you, my God." And when I think of deer...I think of hunting.

I didn't grow up hunting. Neither of my grandfather's hunted. Dad says he's been deer hunting twice in his whole life, and made both in one trip. "How do you accomplish that?", you might ask. Well, Dad has declared it was his first *and* last. He just remembers being cold and miserable above all.

I started hunting some in college, but I've only "gotten serious about it" over the last few years. Believe it or not, Kelly actually likes cooking with venison and that requires that I spend more time in the woods. (Golly bum, I guess I'll just have to take one for the team.) To extend the deer season, I really enjoy hunting with my crossbow.

Hunting with a crossbow is more challenging because you have to get closer to the deer. To accomplish this, I have a homemade camouflage ground blind from which to hunt. It is three, six foot pieces of PVC pipe covered in camouflage duct tape, attached at the top with an old coat hanger and set up like a teepee. We cover the whole thing in camouflage burlap and mesh. I wear camouflage boots, camouflage pants, camouflage shirt, camouflage coat, and even have a camouflage leafy mask to cover my face. I become the woods!

Generally, when I crossbow hunt, I leave my power wheelchair and customized vehicle behind. I use my forearm crutches to climb into a hunting buddy's four-wheel drive truck. Sometimes we drive so far back into the woods that I think perhaps even the deer won't travel that far. After I sit my completely camouflaged self down in the middle of nowhere and my buddy sits up the "tepee of death" around me, they usually cut some foliage to blend me in with the surroundings. Then *they leave me there* to go hunt from another location. Sometimes as they're leaving I'll whisper, "Don't forget where you put me."

Being this well camouflaged has allowed me to get incredibly close to quite a few deer. But, you know what? Never once have I ever heard any of them panting. If you turn a dog loose, they'll pant at the drop of a hat. But a deer? Not so much. The only thing I can figure, is that I've never been close to one that was really as *thirsty* as the one described by the Psalmist.

Why would a deer be so thirsty that it would pant? My only guess would be that it had been running for a long time, and was extremely tired. Dear friend, are you tired of running? Are you tired of chasing after your righteousness in your own wisdom? King Solomon called this "a chasing after the wind".(Ecc. 2:11)

"Blessed are those who hunger and thirst for righteousness, for they will be filled." I pray that we would all become so hungry and so thirsty for the righteousness of God that it becomes our one and only magnificent obsession.

Blessed Are the Pushovers
Matthew 5:5

*T*he story is told about a sheriff's deputy in a rural area watching an intersection, bored to tears on a hot, muggy, July night. Shortly after midnight a car approached the intersection, and, unaware of the deputy's presence, rolled through the stop sign without coming to a complete stop. On a busier night with more goings on in the county, the deputy might have allowed this infraction to be dismissed. But not on this night!

He turned on his blue lights and quickly pulled the offender over to the shoulder of the road. After asking for the man's license and registration, the deputy asked, "Sir, do you realize you failed to come to a complete stop at that intersection back there?" The man replied, "Well, I slowed up. What's the difference?"

At this point the enraged deputy throws open the car door, grabs the guy by the collar, and shoves him to the ground. Then he pulls out his baton and begins to feverishly beat the man about the head and shoulders for what seems like an eternity. The hapless motorist begins to yell, "Stop! Stop! Stop!" To which the deputy responds, "Hey, I got so tired a few minutes ago, I had to slow up…What's the difference?"

Do you know what the guy really wanted? He wanted what all of us deeply desire. What he wanted was mercy. And when we truly realize what a tremendous amount of mercy we've been shown by Holy God, then our only reasonable response has to be a merciful attitude toward others. That is why in Matthew 5:5 Jesus said, "Blessed are the merciful, for they will be shown mercy."

And Then It All Kinda Runs Together
Matthew 5:8-10

"*B*lessed are the pure in heart, for they will see God."(Matt. 5:8) Well, how can that be since none of us are pure in heart? (And if you doubt it, may I refer you to page 25.) Notice how King David responds in Psalm 51 when the prophet Nathan came to him after David had committed adultery with Bathsheba.

> "*Cleanse me* with hyssop, *and I will be clean*; *wash me, and I will be whiter than snow*. Let me hear joy and gladness; let the bones you have crushed rejoice. Hide your face from my sins and blot out all my iniquity. *Create in me a pure heart, O God*, and renew a steadfast spirit within me. Do not cast me from your presence or take your Holy Spirit from me.

Restore to me the joy of your salvation and grant me a willing spirit, to sustain me."

So as to be abundantly clear, those who will see God are those who are pure in heart. And the only way to have a pure heart is for God Himself to make it pure. And He only does that through our trusting in the acceptable sacrifice of His only Son, King Jesus…

"*B*lessed are the peacemakers, for they will be called children of God." Who are the children of God? Well those who've made peace with God, of course. How does this peace occur? It is only when His Holy Spirit fills us with His love. (Refer to page 40.) In Acts 4:8 & 12 we read, "Then Peter, *filled with the Holy Spirit*, said to them: 'Rulers and elders of the people… Salvation is found in *no one else*, for there is *no* *other name* under heaven given to mankind by which we must be saved'."…

"*B*lessed are those who are persecuted because of righteousness, for theirs is the kingdom of heaven." Will you be persecuted? Well, sorta. (See page 62.) Will things be complicated and confusing and troublesome and difficult at times? You bet. But Jesus says in John 16:33…

"I have told you these things, so that in me you may have peace. In this world you will have trouble. But take heart! I have overcome the world."

ABOUT THE AUTHOR

Justin earned both his Bachelor's and Master's Degrees in Agricultural Economics from Mississippi State University. He has been employed in post-secondary education for more than fifteen years. His current position is Economics Instructor at Jefferson State Community College, where in 2004 he received the Phi Theta Kappa Outstanding Faculty Member Award, and in 2008, 2013 & 2014 was nominated for the college's Outstanding Faculty Member Award. Through the years, Justin has traveled to countless speaking engagements to share with others the stories of how God is working in his life. He and Kelly, his wife of eight years, are members of Community Presbyterian Church in Moody, Alabama where they reside with their two children, Will and Anna Morgan.

For booking information, contact justfish419@yahoo.com .